Lquetrip

Santiago

Chile

Edited By:
Elara Fitzroy

Cover By:
Orion Blakeley

First Printing Edition, 2023

ISBN 979-8860555266

Table of Contents

About Our Authors

Seraphina Lane is a respected travel guidebook author known for her captivating exploration narratives. With an insatiable curiosity, she delves beyond conventional travel advice, infusing her writing with the essence of each destination. Seraphina's commitment to responsible travel shines, urging readers to not only discover new places but also embrace cultural understanding. Her guidebooks resonate with both seasoned adventurers and armchair enthusiasts, making her a beacon for those who seek genuine and meaningful travel experiences.

Caspian Frost is an award-winning travel writer and photographer with over 10 years of experience. He has visited over 50 countries on six continents. With a natural flair for storytelling and a genuine passion for exploration, Caspian's writing transcends traditional travel guides. His works are a fusion of practical advice and immersive experiences. Caspian's deep respect for different cultures and environments underscores his approach, advocating for travel that leaves a positive impact. Through his guidebooks, both seasoned globetrotters and armchair travelers find inspiration to uncover the beauty and diversity our world has to offer.

Lo Barnechea

Quilicura

Huech-
uraba

Vitacura

Conchalí

Recoleta

Las Condes

Renca

Independencia

Cerro Navia

Quinta
Normal

Providencia

Pudahuel

La Reina

Lo Prado

Santiago

Ñuñoa

Estación
Central

Peñalolén

Pedro
Aguirre
Cerda

San
Joaquín

Macul

Cerrillos

San
Miguel

Maipú

Lo
Espejo

La
Cisterna

La
Granja

La Florida

San
Ramón

El Bosque

Padre
Hurtado

La Pintana

Puente Alto

San José
de Malpo

San
Bernardo

Pirque

Introduction

Welcome to Santiago, Chile

Santiago, where every street corner holds a story, and every experience promises to leave an indelible mark on your soul. Whether you are a seasoned traveler or a first-time adventurer, this book is designed with you in mind, providing you with a comprehensive and reader-centric companion to discover the hidden gems, iconic landmarks, and unique flavors that define Santiago.

Within these pages, you will find a carefully curated collection of insights, tips, and recommendations, all aimed at ensuring that your visit to Santiago exceeds your expectations. By placing you at the heart of this guide, our mission is to create an immersive and engaging experience that will not only inform but also inspire you to delve deeper into the wonders of this magnificent city.

But why Santiago? Because it is a city that embraces contrasts, seamlessly blending its centuries-old traditions with a modern, cosmopolitan flair. Here, you will witness the harmonious coexistence of historic architecture alongside sleek skyscrapers, and traditional markets bustling with energy alongside fashionable boutiques and designer stores. Santiago pulsates with life, offering a myriad of activities and experiences to satisfy every traveler's desires.

As you journey through these pages, you will discover the must-visit attractions that define Santiago's identity, from the iconic Plaza de Armas and the majestic La Moneda Palace to the enchanting Santa Lucía Hill, where you can immerse yourself in the city's natural beauty. Museums and cultural sites await your exploration, qhich will allow you to delve into the fascinating history and artistic heritage of Chile. And let us not forget the mouthwatering culinary delights that Santiago has to offer—enticing your taste buds with traditional Chilean dishes and international cuisines that reflect the city's diverse influences.

We understand that travel is not just about ticking off landmarks; it is about embracing the essence of a place, connecting with its people, and creating memories that will last a lifetime. That is why this guide goes beyond the usual recommendations, taking you off the beaten path to uncover hidden gems and local secrets. Whether you wish to embark on a wine tasting adventure in the Maipo Valley, embark on a breathtaking hike in the majestic Andes Mountains, or simply lose yourself in the vibrant energy of Santiago's neighborhoods, we have curated an array of experiences to cater to your interests and desires.

Dear reader, let us embark on this captivating journey together. Turn the pages of this guide and let Santiago's charm unfold before your eyes. Immerse yourself in the vibrant culture, explore the streets filled with captivating stories, and savor the flavors that will tantalize your taste buds. Santiago awaits your arrival, ready to enchant and captivate you in ways you never thought possible.

Are you ready?

A Brief History of Santiago

Santiago, the capital city of Chile, has a captivating history that weaves together indigenous cultures, Spanish colonization, and the journey towards independence. Before European explorers arrived, the Picunche and Mapuche indigenous peoples inhabited the region, nurturing their own rich traditions and way of life.

In the year 1541, Santiago's story took a new turn when Spanish conquistador Pedro de Valdivia founded the city of Santiago del Nuevo Extremo. The city was named after Saint James (Santiago) and its remote location within the vast territory. Santiago quickly grew into a significant political and administrative center within the Spanish colonial empire.

During the colonial era, Santiago flourished and witnessed remarkable architectural development. The city's historic center, characterized by its charming colonial buildings, narrow streets, and lively plazas, stands as a testament to its Spanish colonial heritage. The Plaza de Armas, Santiago's main square, became a central gathering place where locals and travelers alike came together to celebrate, converse, and exchange ideas.

The early 19th century marked a crucial period for Santiago and Chile as a whole. The winds of independence swept across Latin America, and on September 18, 1810, Chile declared its first steps towards self-governance through the establishment of the First Government Junta. The journey towards independence was arduous, with Chile enduring years of struggle and conflicts against the Spanish colonial forces.

One pivotal moment in Chile's fight for independence was the Battle of Maipú in 1818. Under the leadership of General Bernardo O'Higgins and Argentine General José de San Martín, Chilean forces achieved a decisive victory against the Spanish army. This triumph marked a turning point in the independence movement, solidifying Chile's path to freedom.

The 19th and 20th centuries brought periods of economic growth, urban expansion, and cultural transformation to Santiago. The city evolved into a bustling commercial and industrial hub, attracting immigrants from various parts of the world, including Europe, the Middle East, and other regions of Latin America. This multicultural influx enriched Santiago's cultural tapestry, leaving a lasting impact on its architecture, cuisine, and traditions.

In recent years, Santiago has experienced significant urban development, with the construction of modern skyscrapers, improved infrastructure, and enhanced public transportation. The city has embraced its cosmopolitan nature, boasting a thriving arts scene, innovative culinary experiences, and renowned educational institutions.

Today, Santiago proudly stands as Chile's political, cultural, and economic capital. It honors its past while embracing the opportunities and challenges of the present. Visitors to Santiago can explore its fascinating history through its museums, historic sites, and vibrant neighborhoods, providing a glimpse into the city's rich heritage and the resilience of its people.

As you wander through the streets of Santiago, allow the city's storied past to guide you. Discover the layers of its history and let the spirit of Santiago envelop you, offering an unforgettable experience that is truly unique to this remarkable destination.

Climate and Best Time to Visit

Santiago, Chile is a city that experiences a Mediterranean climate, with warm, dry summers and cool, wet winters. The average temperature in Santiago ranges from 10 degrees Celsius in winter to 26 degrees Celsius in summer. The driest months are from October to April, and the wettest months are from May to September.

The best time to visit Santiago is during the shoulder seasons, from September to November and from March to May. The weather is mild during these months, with plenty of sunshine and not too many crowds. However, it is important to note that the shoulder seasons can still be quite hot, especially in September and October.

If you are planning to visit Santiago during the summer, be prepared for hot, humid weather. The average temperature in Santiago during the summer is 26 degrees Celsius, and the humidity can be high. If you are not used to hot weather, you may want to consider visiting Santiago during the shoulder seasons.

If you are planning to visit Santiago during the winter, be prepared for cool, wet weather. The average temperature in Santiago during the winter is 10 degrees Celsius, and it can rain or snow frequently. If you are not used to cold weather, you may want to pack warm clothes and rain gear.

Here are some additional tips for planning your trip to Santiago, Chile:

- **Choose the right clothes.** The climate in Santiago varies greatly from season to season, so it is important to pack clothes that are appropriate for the weather. For example, if you are visiting Santiago in the summer, you will need to pack light, loose-fitting clothing made of breathable fabrics. If you are visiting Santiago in the winter, you will need to pack warm clothes and rain gear.
- **Get a visa.** If you are not a citizen of Chile, you will need to get a visa before you travel. You can apply for a visa online or at a Chilean embassy or consulate.
- **Take out travel insurance.** Travel insurance can help to protect you financially in the event of an accident, illness, or other unforeseen event.
- **Learn some basic Spanish phrases.** It is helpful to learn some basic Spanish phrases before you travel to Santiago. This will help you to communicate with locals and get around more easily.
- **Be prepared for altitude sickness.** Santiago is located at an altitude of over 2,800 meters, so some people may

experience altitude sickness. Symptoms of altitude sickness include headache, nausea, vomiting, and dizziness. If you are experiencing any of these symptoms, it is important to descend to a lower altitude as soon as possible.

- **Have fun!** Santiago is a fascinating and diverse city with something to offer everyone. So relax, enjoy the journey, and soak up the sights, sounds, and smells of Santiago.

LOQUETRIP

Getting to Santiago

International Flights to Santiago

Santiago is a popular tourist destination and is served by several international airlines. The most popular airlines that fly to Santiago from the United States are LATAM Airlines, American Airlines, and Delta Air Lines. These airlines offer direct flights from major US cities such as New York, Los Angeles, and Miami.

The flight time from the United States to Santiago varies depending on the departure city. The shortest flight time is from Miami, which is about 5 hours and 30 minutes. The longest flight time is from New York, which is about 10 hours and 30 minutes.

The average cost of an international flight to Santiago from the United States varies depending on the time of year and the departure city. The cheapest flights can be found during the shoulder seasons, which are September to November and March to May. The most expensive flights can be found during the peak season, which is December to February.

Here are some tips for finding cheap flights to Santiago:

- **Book your flight in advance.** The earlier you book, the more likely you are to find a good deal.

- **Be flexible with your travel dates.** If you can, try to fly on weekdays or during off-peak hours.
- **Consider flying into a different airport.** If you are willing to fly into a smaller airport, you may be able to find cheaper flights.
- **Use a flight search engine.** There are a number of flight search engines available online that can help you compare prices and find the best deals.

Once you have booked your flight, you will need to apply for a visa if you are not a citizen of Chile. You can apply for a visa online or at a Chilean embassy or consulate.

Here are some tips for getting to and from the airport in Santiago:

- The most convenient way to get to and from the airport is by taxi. Taxis are relatively inexpensive in Santiago.
- If you are on a budget, you can take the metro to the airport. The metro is a quick and affordable way to get to and from the airport.
- There are also a number of shuttle services that operate between the airport and the city center. Shuttle services are a good option if you are traveling with a group of people.

Domestic Transportation Options

When it comes to exploring the sprawling city of Santiago, having a good understanding of the available domestic transportation options is essential. Santiago's vast size and diverse attractions make it crucial to choose the right mode of transportation to navigate the city efficiently. Here, we delve into the various transportation options, providing you with fresh insights and information.

Metro

The Santiago Metro system is the backbone of the city's transportation network. It is widely regarded as one of the most efficient, clean, and affordable ways to travel within Santiago. With six lines and over 130 stations, the metro covers extensive areas, connecting major attractions and neighborhoods. Whether you're heading to the historic city center or exploring the bohemian charm of Bellavista, the metro offers a convenient and reliable option.

Bus

Buses are a popular choice for both locals and visitors looking to traverse Santiago. The city boasts a range of bus companies that operate diverse routes, allowing for flexibility in reaching destinations not covered by the metro. Buses are an economical option, ideal for budget-conscious travelers. However, it's worth noting that buses can be slower and more crowded, particularly during peak hours.

Taxi

Taxis provide a convenient and door-to-door transportation experience in Santiago. They are readily available throughout the city, and you can easily flag one down or find them at designated taxi stands. While taxis offer a more personalized and comfortable journey, it's important to keep in mind that fares can be relatively higher compared to other options. Taxis operate on a metered system, with fares starting around 700 Chilean pesos, which is approximately $1 USD.

Uber and Ride-Sharing

Uber, the well-known ride-sharing service, operates in Santiago and has gained popularity among locals and tourists alike. Using the Uber app, you can request a ride and enjoy the convenience of door-to-door service at competitive rates. Similar to taxis,

Uber provides a comfortable and reliable transportation option, particularly if you prefer the convenience of app-based services.

Car Rental

Renting a car offers flexibility and freedom for those wishing to explore Santiago and its surrounding areas independently. However, it's important to consider the traffic congestion that often plagues the city, especially during peak hours. If you plan to venture outside the city or have specific destinations in mind, renting a car can be a practical choice. Keep in mind that parking can be a challenge in certain areas, and familiarizing yourself with local driving rules and regulations is essential.

When deciding on the right domestic transportation option in Santiago, consider various factors. Your budget, the time of day, your destination, and your personal comfort level all play a role in determining the best mode of transportation for your needs. Whether you opt for the efficiency of the metro, the affordability of buses, the convenience of taxis and ride-sharing services, or the freedom of a rental car, Santiago provides a range of options to suit every traveler's preferences and requirements.

Traveling within the City

Santiago is a large and spread-out city, so it is important to have a good understanding of the different transportation options available. Here are some of the most popular ways to travel within the city:

- **Metro**

As mentioned in the last section, The metro is the most efficient and affordable way to get around Santiago. It is a fast, clean, and safe way to travel, and it covers most of the city. The metro has six lines and over 130 stations. Tickets can be purchased at vending machines or at the ticket booth at each station.

- **Bus**

Buses are another popular way to get around Santiago. There are a variety of bus companies that operate in the city, and they offer a wide range of services. Buses are a good option if you are traveling on a budget, but they can be more crowded and slower than the metro.

- **Taxi**

Taxis are a convenient way to get around Santiago, but they can be expensive.

- **Uber**

Uber is a popular ride-hailing service that is available in Santiago. Uber is a good option if you are looking for a more affordable alternative to taxis.

- **Walking**

Walking is a great way to explore Santiago at your own pace. The city is relatively flat, and there are plenty of sidewalks and crosswalks. Walking is a good option if you are on a budget and want to get some exercise.

- **Biking**

Biking is a great way to get around Santiago and see the city from a different perspective. There are a number of bike paths and lanes available, and the traffic is not as heavy as it is in some other cities. Biking is a good option if you are looking for a healthy and active way to get around.

Here are some tips for traveling within the city of Santiago:

- **Purchase a bip! card.** A bip! card is a rechargeable card that can be used on the metro, bus, and some taxis. It is a more convenient and affordable way to pay for transportation.
- **Plan your route.** Before you set out, take a look at a map of the city and plan your route. This will help you avoid getting lost and save time.
- **Be aware of your surroundings.** Santiago is a safe city, but it is always a good idea to be aware of your surroundings, especially at night.
- **Use common sense.** Do not leave your belongings unattended, and be careful when carrying large sums of money.

Accommodation

Neighborhoods in Santiago

Santiago is a city brimming with diverse neighborhoods, each with its unique character and charm. From historic districts that echo with stories of the past to vibrant modern enclaves pulsating with contemporary energy, Santiago's neighborhoods offer a kaleidoscope of experiences for visitors to explore. Here, we uncover some of the captivating neighborhoods that make Santiago a truly captivating destination.

Bellavista

Nestled at the foot of San Cristóbal Hill, Bellavista is Santiago's bohemian heart. This artistic neighborhood exudes an eclectic and vibrant atmosphere, with its colorful streets lined with art galleries, theaters, and trendy cafés. Bellavista is also home to La Chascona, the former residence of Chilean poet Pablo Neruda, which now serves as a museum dedicated to his life and works. By day, you can explore the unique boutiques and immerse yourself in the neighborhood's creative energy, while by night, Bellavista transforms into a hub of nightlife, with its lively bars and clubs filling the streets with music and revelry.

Lastarria

Located in the heart of Santiago, Lastarria is a neighborhood known for its picturesque streets, charming architecture, and vibrant cultural scene. This bohemian enclave is dotted with art galleries, museums, and theaters, making it a haven for art enthusiasts and history buffs. Lastarria is also home to the Centro Cultural Gabriela Mistral (GAM), a contemporary arts center that hosts exhibitions, performances, and cultural events. With its tree-lined avenues, quaint cafés, and a wide array of culinary delights, Lastarria invites you to leisurely stroll through its streets, savoring its artistic ambiance and soaking in the lively atmosphere.

Providencia

Providencia is a bustling and upscale neighborhood that seamlessly blends residential areas, commercial districts, and recreational spaces. Known for its wide tree-lined avenues and modern architecture, Providencia offers a vibrant shopping scene, with high-end boutiques and shopping malls catering to fashion-forward locals and visitors. The neighborhood is also home to numerous parks and green spaces, such as Parque de las Esculturas and Parque Metropolitano, where you can enjoy outdoor activities and take in panoramic views of the city. Providencia's culinary scene is equally enticing, with a plethora of trendy restaurants, cafés, and bars offering a wide range of international and local flavors.

Barrio Italia

For those seeking a bohemian and artistic ambiance, Barrio Italia is a must-visit neighborhood in Santiago. This charming district is characterized by its narrow streets lined with quaint houses that have been transformed into unique boutiques, antique shops, art galleries, and design studios. Barrio Italia's creative spirit is palpable as you wander through its colorful alleyways, discovering hidden gems and one-of-a-kind crafts. The neighborhood also boasts a vibrant café culture, where you can relax, sip a cup of locally roasted coffee, and soak in the neighborhood's creative energy.

La Reina

Nestled at the foothills of the Andes Mountains, La Reina offers a suburban retreat from the hustle and bustle of central Santiago. This tranquil and residential neighborhood is characterized by its spacious streets, parks, and green areas, providing a peaceful escape for residents and visitors alike. La Reina is home to Parque Mahuida, a vast natural park offering hiking trails, picnic areas, and stunning panoramic views of Santiago. The neighborhood also boasts a rich cultural heritage, with historic sites such as the Iglesia de La Reina, a beautiful church that stands as a testament to the area's history.

These are just a few of the neighborhoods that define Santiago's diverse tapestry. Each neighborhood offers its unique blend of history, culture, and experiences, inviting you to uncover the hidden treasures that make Santiago a captivating destination. So, immerse yourself in the vibrant streets, explore the local hotspots, and embrace the distinctive flavors of each neighborhood, as you embark on a journey to discover the true soul of Santiago.

Types of Accommodations

When visiting Santiago, Chile, finding the right accommodation is crucial for a comfortable and enjoyable stay. The city offers a diverse range of accommodations to suit every traveler's needs and preferences. From luxurious hotels to budget-friendly hostels and cozy vacation rentals, Santiago provides options that cater to various budgets and travel styles. Here, we explore the different types of accommodations available in Santiago:

Hotels

Santiago boasts a wide selection of hotels, ranging from luxurious five-star establishments to more affordable boutique hotels. The city's upscale hotels offer an array of amenities, including spa facilities, rooftop pools, gourmet restaurants, and stunning views of the city skyline. Many hotels are conveniently located in key areas such as the city center or upscale neighborhoods like Providencia, allowing easy access to major attractions, shopping districts, and dining options. For those seeking a more personalized experience, boutique hotels offer unique charm and character, often with fewer rooms and a more intimate atmosphere.

Hostels

Hostels provide a budget-friendly option for travelers, especially for those seeking a social and communal atmosphere. Santiago offers a variety of hostels that cater to solo travelers, backpackers, and groups. These accommodations often feature dormitory-style rooms with shared facilities, such as communal kitchens, common areas, and organized activities. Hostels are not only an affordable choice but also a great way to meet fellow travelers and exchange experiences and tips.

Vacation Rentals

Vacation rentals, such as apartments or houses, have gained popularity among travelers looking for a home-away-from-home experience. Santiago offers a range of vacation rental options, from cozy apartments in the city center to spacious houses in residential neighborhoods. Vacation rentals provide the convenience of having your own space, kitchen facilities, and the opportunity to live like a local. They are particularly suitable for families or groups who prefer more privacy and flexibility during their stay.

Bed and Breakfasts

For a charming and intimate experience, bed and breakfasts (B&Bs) in Santiago offer a cozy and personalized stay. B&Bs often feature comfortable rooms with breakfast included in the rate. These accommodations are typically located in residential areas or historic districts, providing a glimpse into local life and culture. B&B hosts often provide insider tips and recommendations to enhance your visit to Santiago.

Apart Hotels

Apart hotels offer a blend of hotel-like services and the convenience of a self-catering apartment. These accommodations typically feature furnished apartments with kitchenettes or full kitchens, allowing guests to prepare their meals. Apart hotels often provide amenities such as housekeeping, reception services, and sometimes access to fitness facilities or swimming pools. They are a popular choice for extended stays or for travelers who prefer a more independent and flexible accommodation option.

When choosing the right accommodation in Santiago, consider factors such as location, budget, amenities, and the type of experience you desire. Whether you prefer the luxury and pampering of a hotel, the social ambiance of a hostel, the comfort of a vacation rental, the charm of a bed and breakfast, or the convenience of an apart hotel, Santiago offers a wide range of choices to suit every traveler's preferences. Take your time to explore the options and find the perfect accommodation that will enhance your stay in this captivating city.

Budget Options

When traveling to Santiago, Chile, budget-conscious travelers will be pleased to find a range of affordable accommodations that provide comfort and convenience without breaking the bank. Santiago offers several budget-friendly options that allow you to make the most of your travel funds while enjoying a comfortable stay. Here, we explore some of the budget accommodation choices available in the city:

Hostels

Hostels are a popular choice for budget travelers in Santiago. They offer affordable dormitory-style rooms with shared facilities such as bathrooms, kitchens, and common areas. Hostels provide a social atmosphere where you can meet fellow travelers and exchange experiences and tips. Many hostels in Santiago also offer private rooms for those seeking more privacy while still keeping costs low. With various locations throughout the city, hostels provide convenient access to attractions, public transportation, and dining options.

Budget Hotels

Santiago has a selection of budget hotels that offer comfortable accommodations at affordable prices. These hotels provide well-maintained rooms with essential amenities, ensuring a pleasant stay without the frills of higher-end establishments. While they may not offer the same range of facilities as luxury hotels, budget hotels in Santiago still prioritize cleanliness, friendly service, and convenient locations. They serve as a great base for exploring the city while keeping costs in check.

Guesthouses and Bed and Breakfasts

Guesthouses and bed and breakfasts are another cost-effective option for accommodation in Santiago. These smaller establishments often offer comfortable rooms with a homely atmosphere. Many guesthouses and bed and breakfasts provide breakfast as part of the room rate, allowing you to start your day with a satisfying meal. They are typically located in residential areas or quieter neighborhoods, offering a chance to experience local life and culture.

Vacation Rentals

Vacation rentals can be an excellent choice for budget travelers, particularly for those traveling in groups or for an extended period. Renting an apartment or house allows you to have a home-away-from-home experience while enjoying the freedom to cook your meals and live like a local. Santiago offers a range of affordable vacation rental options throughout the city, providing comfort, privacy, and the flexibility to manage your budget effectively.

Camping

For nature enthusiasts and those seeking a unique budget experience, camping is a possibility in and around Santiago. There are several campgrounds and outdoor recreational areas near the city where you can pitch your tent or rent camping facilities. Camping provides an affordable and immersive way to connect with nature while still having access to the amenities and attractions of Santiago.

When selecting budget accommodations in Santiago, it's essential to consider factors such as location, safety, and reviews from previous guests. Researching different options, comparing prices, and reading traveler reviews can help you find the best budget option that suits your needs and preferences.

Budget Option Hostels in Santiago

- **Hostel Bellavista**

Hostel Bellavista is a great option for budget travelers. It is located in the trendy Bellavista neighborhood, close to many restaurants, bars, and museums. The hostel offers basic but clean rooms with shared bathrooms. There is also a communal kitchen where guests can prepare their own meals.

- **Hostel S&G**

Hostel S&G is a good option for budget travelers who are looking for a relaxed and social atmosphere. It is located in the Providencia neighborhood, close to many restaurants, bars, and shops. The hostel offers comfortable rooms with shared bathrooms. There is also a large communal kitchen and a terrace where guests can relax and socialize.

- **Landay Hostel**

Landay Hostel is a bright and airy hostel located in the heart of Santiago. It offers a variety of room options, including shared dormitories, private rooms, and family rooms. The hostel also has a communal kitchen, a laundry room, and a roof terrace with stunning views of the city.

- **Ají Hostel**

Ají Hostel is a simple but stylish hostel located in the Providencia neighborhood. It offers a variety of room options, including shared dormitories, private rooms, and family rooms. The hostel also has a communal kitchen, a laundry room, and a rooftop terrace with a barbecue.

- **EcoHostel**

EcoHostel is an eco-friendly hostel located in the Providencia neighborhood. It offers a variety of room options, including shared dormitories, private rooms, and family rooms. The hostel also has a communal kitchen, a laundry room, and a rooftop terrace with a swimming pool.

Mid-Range Options

Santiago, Chile offers a variety of mid-range accommodations that strike a balance between comfort and affordability, allowing travelers to enjoy a pleasant stay without stretching their budget too thin. These mid-range options provide a range of amenities and services that enhance the overall experience while ensuring good value for your money. Here, we explore some of the mid-range accommodation choices available in Santiago:

Mid-Range Hotels: Santiago boasts numerous mid-range hotels that provide a higher level of comfort and service compared to budget accommodations. These hotels offer well-appointed rooms with amenities such as private bathrooms, Wi-Fi access, and in-room entertainment. Many mid-range hotels also feature on-site restaurants, fitness centers, and 24-hour reception services. They often have convenient locations, allowing easy access to popular attractions, dining options, and public transportation.

Boutique Hotels: For those seeking a more unique and intimate experience, boutique hotels in Santiago offer a charming and personalized stay. These smaller establishments typically feature stylish décor, distinctive themes, and a cozy ambiance. Boutique hotels often prioritize attentive service and provide amenities such as complimentary breakfast, cozy common areas, and personalized recommendations for exploring the city. They offer an opportunity to immerse yourself in a more intimate atmosphere while enjoying the comfort and convenience of mid-range accommodations.

Aparthotels: Aparthotels combine the convenience of a hotel with the added flexibility of a self-contained apartment. These accommodations feature spacious units with separate living and sleeping areas, along with kitchen facilities that allow you to prepare your meals. Aparthotels typically offer additional amenities such as housekeeping, on-site laundry facilities, and sometimes access to fitness centers or swimming pools. They are an excellent option for travelers who value the independence and freedom of having their own space while still enjoying hotel-like services.

Guesthouses and Bed and Breakfasts: Guesthouses and bed and breakfasts in the mid-range category provide comfortable accommodations with a personal touch. These establishments often feature well-appointed rooms with private bathrooms and common areas where you can relax and mingle with other guests. Guesthouses and bed and breakfasts typically offer a hearty breakfast as part of the room rate and may provide additional services such as airport transfers or tour arrangements. They provide a warm and welcoming atmosphere that adds a sense of home to your stay in Santiago.

Serviced Apartments: Serviced apartments are another mid-range option that offers the comforts of home combined with hotel-like services. These accommodations provide fully furnished apartments with separate living spaces, kitchen facilities, and often additional amenities like on-site laundry facilities or fitness centers. Serviced apartments are ideal for travelers who value privacy and prefer the flexibility of a self-catering option. They are particularly suitable for longer stays or for those traveling with families or larger groups.

When selecting mid-range accommodations in Santiago, consider factors such as location, amenities, and the level of service offered. Read reviews from previous guests to get a sense of the overall experience. By choosing one of these mid-range options, you can enjoy a comfortable and well-rounded stay in Santiago, striking the right balance between affordability and the added comforts that enhance your overall travel experience.

Here are some of the Mid-Range Options in Santiago

- **CasaSur Recoleta**

CasaSur Recoleta is a stylish boutique hotel located in the trendy Recoleta neighborhood. The hotel offers comfortable rooms with air conditioning, Wi-Fi, and minibars. There is also a rooftop terrace with stunning views of the city.

CasaSur Providencia is another stylish boutique hotel located in the Providencia neighborhood. The hotel offers comfortable rooms with air conditioning, Wi-Fi, and minibars. There is also a rooftop terrace with a pool and barbecue facilities.

- **Hotel Magnolia**

Hotel Magnolia is a good option for mid-range travelers who are looking for a more traditional hotel. It is located in the heart of the city, close to many tourist attractions. The hotel offers spacious rooms with air conditioning, Wi-Fi, and minibars. There is also a breakfast buffet available for an additional charge.

Hotel CasaSur Los Leones is a good option for mid-range travelers who are looking for a more luxurious stay. It is located in the prestigious Los Leones neighborhood, close to many embassies and businesses. The hotel offers stylish rooms with air conditioning, Wi-Fi, and minibars. There is also a rooftop pool and bar with stunning views of the city.

- **Apart Hotel Terraza Bellavista**

Apart Hotel Terraza Bellavista is a great option for mid-range travelers who are looking for an apartment-style hotel. It is located in the trendy Bellavista neighborhood, close to many restaurants, bars, and museums. The hotel offers spacious apartments with fully equipped kitchens, living rooms, and dining areas. There is also a rooftop terrace with a pool and barbecue facilities.

- **Apart Hotel One Providencia**

Apart Hotel One Providencia is a great option for mid-range travelers who are looking for an apartment-style hotel in the Providencia neighborhood. The hotel offers spacious apartments with fully equipped kitchens, living rooms, and dining areas. There is also a rooftop terrace with a pool and barbecue facilities.

These are just a few of the many mid-range accommodations options in Santiago. When choosing a mid-range hotel, it is important to consider your needs and budget. If you are looking for a comfortable and stylish stay, then a boutique hotel will be a good option. If you are looking for an apartment-style hotel, then an apart hotel will be a better choice.

Luxury Options

Santiago offers a range of luxurious accommodations that cater to discerning travelers seeking the finest amenities, personalized service, and an unforgettable experience. These luxury options in Santiago redefine hospitality, providing opulent surroundings, world-class facilities, and impeccable attention to detail. Here, we explore some of the luxurious accommodation choices available in Santiago:

Luxury Hotels: Santiago boasts a collection of prestigious luxury hotels that epitomize elegance and sophistication. These five-star establishments offer a wealth of amenities, including spacious and beautifully appointed rooms, luxurious bedding, stunning city or mountain views, and state-of-the-art technology. Pampering spa facilities, fitness centers, gourmet restaurants, and stylish bars are often part of the package. Luxury hotels in Santiago focus on delivering exceptional service, ensuring that every aspect of your stay is tailored to your needs and preferences.

Boutique Hotels: For those seeking a more intimate and exclusive experience, Santiago's boutique hotels provide a luxurious escape. These small, independent properties offer personalized service, unique architectural design, and meticulous attention to detail. Boutique hotels in Santiago often feature individually decorated rooms with high-quality furnishings, lavish bathrooms, and upscale amenities. They provide a tranquil oasis amidst the bustling city, allowing you to immerse yourself in a world of refined luxury.

Spa Retreats: Santiago is home to several spa retreats that provide a haven of relaxation and rejuvenation. These luxury accommodations focus on wellness and offer an array of spa treatments, wellness programs, and fitness facilities. From indulgent massages to revitalizing facials and holistic therapies, spa retreats in Santiago ensure a pampering experience for the mind, body, and soul. Immerse yourself in a sanctuary of tranquility and let the stresses of daily life melt away in the lap of luxury.

High-End Serviced Apartments: For travelers seeking the comforts of home combined with the convenience of hotel services, high-end serviced apartments in Santiago offer the perfect solution. These luxurious apartments feature spacious living areas, fully equipped kitchens, and upscale amenities. You can enjoy the privacy and flexibility of a self-contained residence while benefiting from hotel-like services such as housekeeping, 24-hour concierge, and in-room dining. High-end serviced apartments provide a refined and exclusive experience for those seeking an elevated level of comfort.

Luxury Resorts: Located just outside the city, luxury resorts provide a secluded retreat with lavish amenities and breathtaking surroundings. These resorts often offer expansive grounds, lush gardens, and panoramic views of the surrounding landscapes. Facilities such as swimming pools, spa and wellness centers, fine dining restaurants, and recreational activities are available to ensure an indulgent and memorable stay. Luxury resorts near Santiago allow you to experience the tranquility of nature while enjoying the finest hospitality and a range of leisure options.

When choosing luxury accommodations in Santiago, consider factors such as location, reputation, and the specific amenities that align with your preferences. Each luxurious option in Santiago strives to create an exceptional experience, combining elegance, comfort, and personalized service to ensure that every moment of your stay is truly extraordinary.

Here are some of the Luxury Options in Santiago

- ### Hotel The Singular

The Singular is a luxurious hotel located in the heart of Santiago. The hotel offers stylish rooms with air conditioning, Wi-Fi, and minibars. There is also a rooftop pool and bar with stunning views of the city. The Singular also has a spa, a fitness center, and a sauna.

- ### Hotel W Santiago

The W Santiago is a modern and stylish hotel located in the upscale Vitacura neighborhood. The hotel offers spacious rooms with air conditioning, Wi-Fi, and minibars. There is also a rooftop pool and bar with stunning views of the city. The W Santiago also has a spa, a fitness center, and a nightclub.

- ### Hotel Ritz-Carlton, Santiago

The Ritz-Carlton, Santiago is a luxurious hotel located in the heart of Santiago. The hotel offers elegant rooms with air conditioning, Wi-Fi, and minibars. There is also a rooftop pool and bar with stunning views of the city. The Ritz-Carlton, Santiago also has a spa, a fitness center, and a golf course.

- **Hotel Four Seasons, Santiago**

The Four Seasons, Santiago is a luxurious hotel located in the prestigious Vitacura neighborhood. The hotel offers spacious rooms with air conditioning, Wi-Fi, and minibars. There is also a rooftop pool and bar with stunning views of the city. The Four Seasons, Santiago also has a spa, a fitness center, and a tennis court.

- **Hotel Hyatt Centric Las Condes**

The Hyatt Centric Las Condes is a stylish hotel located in the upscale Las Condes neighborhood. The hotel offers comfortable rooms with air conditioning, Wi-Fi, and minibars. There is also a rooftop pool and bar with stunning views of the city. The Hyatt Centric Las Condes also has a spa, a fitness center, and a business center.

These are just a few of the many luxury accommodations options in Santiago. When choosing a luxury hotel, it is important to consider your needs and budget. If you are looking for a stylish and comfortable stay, then a hotel in the Providencia or Las Condes neighborhoods will be a good option. If you are looking for a more traditional and luxurious stay, then a hotel in the Centro Historico neighborhood will be a better choice.

Exploring Santiago

Plaza de Armas

Plaza de Armas, located in the heart of Santiago, Chile, is a historic and cultural hub that serves as the city's main square. Steeped in history and surrounded by iconic landmarks, Plaza de Armas is a vibrant gathering place that offers a glimpse into  Santiago's rich heritage. Here, we delve into the unique features and significance of this captivating square.

Historical Significance

Plaza de Armas holds great historical importance as it was founded in 1541 by Spanish conquistador Pedro de Valdivia, making it one of the oldest public spaces in Santiago. The square served as the focal point of the colonial city, acting as a hub for social, cultural, and political activities. Throughout the centuries, Plaza de Armas witnessed numerous historical events, including independence celebrations and political gatherings, shaping the destiny of Chile.

Architectural Splendor

The square is characterized by its stunning architectural diversity, showcasing a blend of styles from different eras. The surrounding buildings reflect Santiago's history, with influences ranging from Spanish colonial to neoclassical and modernist designs. Notable structures include the Metropolitan Cathedral, the Central Post Office building, the Royal Court Palace, and the National Historical Museum. These architectural gems add to the allure of Plaza de Armas, creating a captivating and picturesque setting.

La Moneda Palace

Situated near Plaza de Armas is the renowned La Moneda Palace, Chile's presidential palace. This architectural masterpiece has witnessed significant moments in Chilean history. Originally a colonial mint, it later became the presidential residence and government seat. Visitors can admire the palace's grand façade and explore its surrounding gardens. La Moneda Palace represents the country's political power and offers a glimpse into Chile's democratic heritage.

Cultural Center

Plaza de Armas is not only a historic site but also a cultural center that celebrates the arts and traditions of Santiago. Street performers, artists, and artisans frequently gather in the square, showcasing their talents and crafts. Visitors can enjoy live music, dance performances, and browse through local handicrafts. The square often hosts cultural events, fairs, and exhibitions, creating a lively and vibrant atmosphere that celebrates Santiago's cultural richness.

Social Gathering Place

Plaza de Armas has long been a social gathering place for locals and visitors alike. It serves as a meeting point, where friends gather, families enjoy leisurely strolls, and people-watching becomes a favorite pastime. The square's central location, surrounded by shops, cafés, and restaurants, makes it an ideal spot to relax, savor a cup of Chilean coffee, and immerse oneself in the city's vibrant energy.

Historical Monuments

Within Plaza de Armas, visitors can admire several statues and monuments that commemorate important figures and events in Chilean history. The equestrian statue of Pedro de Valdivia, the founder of Santiago, stands proudly in the square. Additionally, the monument honoring the indigenous leader Caupolicán symbolizes the cultural diversity and indigenous heritage of Chile.

Plaza de Armas embodies the soul of Santiago, encapsulating its rich history, architectural splendor, cultural vibrancy, and social essence. Whether you are exploring the surrounding historical buildings, witnessing a lively street performance, or simply savoring the ambiance of this bustling square, Plaza de Armas invites you to immerse yourself in Santiago's past and present, serving as a testament to the city's enduring heritage.

Practical Information

Location: Plaza de Armas is located in the heart of Santiago, Chile. It is bordered by the Catedral Metropolitana on the north, the Palacio de La Moneda on the west, the Municipalidad de Santiago on the south, and the Palacio de los Tribunales on the east.

Opening Hours: Plaza de Armas is open to the public 24 hours a day, 7 days a week. However, the Catedral Metropolitana is only open to the public from 9:00 AM to 6:00 PM, and the Palacio de La Moneda is only open to the public from 9:00 AM to 5:00 PM.

Admission Fees: There is no admission fee to visit Plaza de Armas. However, there is an admission fee to visit the Catedral Metropolitana and the Palacio de La Moneda.

Accessibility: Plaza de Armas is wheelchair accessible. There are ramps and elevators to all of the buildings that surround the plaza.

Facilities and Amenities: Plaza de Armas has a number of facilities and amenities, including:

- A variety of restaurants and cafes

- A number of shops
- A public bathroom
- A tourist information center
- A number of benches and chairs where you can relax and enjoy the view

Guided Tours: There are a number of guided tours that are available for Plaza de Armas and the surrounding area. These tours can be a great way to learn more about the history and culture of Santiago.

Safety Guidelines: Plaza de Armas is a safe place to visit. However, it is always important to be aware of your surroundings and take precautions against petty theft.

Nearby Services: There are a number of nearby services available, including:

- Banks
- ATMs
- Restaurants
- Cafes
- Shops
- Hotels
- Hostels

Best Time to Visit: The best time to visit Plaza de Armas is during the day, when the sun is shining and the plaza is bustling with activity. However, Plaza de Armas is also a beautiful place to visit at night, when the buildings are illuminated.

Contact Information: If you need more information about Plaza de Armas, you can contact the tourist information center located in the plaza. The tourist information center is open from 9:00 AM to 6:00 PM, 7 days a week.

Here are insider tips for visiting Plaza de Armas:

- **Visit the Catedral Metropolitana.** The Catedral Metropolitana is a beautiful cathedral that is located on the north side of Plaza de Armas. The cathedral is free to visit and is open from 9:00 AM to 6:00 PM, 7 days a week.

- **Take a walk around the Palacio de La Moneda.** The Palacio de La Moneda is the presidential palace of Chile. The palace is located on the west side of Plaza de Armas and is open to the public for tours from 9:00 AM to 5:00 PM, 7 days a week.

- **Visit the Municipalidad de Santiago.** The Municipalidad de Santiago is the city hall of Santiago. The building is located on the south side of Plaza de Armas and is open to the public for tours from 9:00 AM to 6:00 PM, 7 days a week.

- **Visit the Palacio de los Tribunales.** The Palacio de los Tribunales is the Supreme Court of Chile. The building is located on the east side of Plaza de Armas and is open to the public for tours from 9:00 AM to 5:00 PM, 7 days a week.

- **Take a guided tour of Plaza de Armas.** There are a number of guided tours that are available for Plaza de

Armas and the surrounding area. These tours can be a great way to learn more about the history and culture of Santiago.

- **Enjoy the food and drink at one of the many restaurants or cafes in Plaza de Armas.** There are a variety of restaurants and cafes to choose from, so you're sure to find something to your taste.
- **Shop at one of the many shops in Plaza de Armas.** There are a variety of shops to choose from, so you're sure to find something you'll love.
- **Relax on one of the benches or chairs in Plaza de Armas.** Plaza de Armas is a great place to relax and people-watch.
- **Attend a cultural event in Plaza de Armas.** There are often cultural events held in Plaza de Armas, such as concerts, festivals, and art exhibitions.
- **Take a photo of Plaza de Armas.**

La Moneda Palace

La Moneda Palace is a historic and iconic building in Santiago, Chile. It has served as the presidential palace of Chile since the 19th century and is a symbol of the country's democratic heritage.

The palace was originally built as a mint in 1805 and was known as Casa de Moneda (House of Currency). In 1845, it was converted into the presidential palace. The palace has witnessed many significant events in Chile's history, including the 1973 military coup that overthrew President Salvador Allende.

La Moneda Palace is a beautiful example of neoclassical architecture. The exterior of the palace is made of white stone and is decorated with statues and reliefs. The interior of the palace is just as impressive, with ornate rooms and halls. The palace also houses a number of important government offices, including the offices of the President, the Cabinet, and the National Congress.

La Moneda Palace is open to the public for tours. Visitors can learn about the history of the palace and see some of the rooms that are used by the President and other government officials. Tours are available in Spanish and English.

Here are some interesting facts about La Moneda Palace:

- The palace was designed by Italian architect Joaquín Toesca.
- The palace is made of white stone and is decorated with a number of statues and reliefs.
- The interior of the palace is just as impressive, with ornate rooms and halls.
- The palace houses a number of important government offices, including the offices of the President, the Cabinet, and the National Congress.
- La Moneda Palace has been the scene of many important events in Chilean history, including the 1973 military coup that overthrew President Salvador Allende.
- La Moneda Palace is open to the public for tours.

Here are some tips for visiting La Moneda Palace:

- The palace is open to the public for tours from 9:00 AM to 5:00 PM, 7 days a week.
- Tours are available in Spanish and English.
- There is a small entrance fee for tours.
- The palace is located in the heart of Santiago, Chile.
- The nearest metro station is the Plaza de Armas station.
- The palace is wheelchair accessible.

Visiting La Moneda Palace is a unique opportunity to learn about Chile's history and culture. The palace is a beautiful and impressive building that is full of history. Tours are available in both Spanish and English, so visitors can learn about the palace in their preferred language.

Santa Lucía Hill

Santa Lucía Hill, located in the heart of Santiago, Chile, is a historic landmark and a cherished urban oasis that offers a breathtaking panoramic view of the city. This prominent hill has a rich history and is a beloved destination for both locals and visitors. Here, we delve into the unique features and cultural significance of Santa Lucía Hill.

Historical Significance

Santa Lucía Hill holds great historical importance as it was originally a sacred site for the indigenous Mapuche people before the arrival of the Spanish. In 1541, Spanish conquistador Pedro de Valdivia claimed the hill and built a fortress, establishing Santiago. Over the centuries, the hill witnessed various transformations, including the addition of gardens, fountains, and architectural elements, shaping it into the picturesque park it is today.

Architectural Beauty

Santa Lucía Hill is renowned for its stunning architecture and beautifully landscaped gardens. The hill features several architectural structures and landmarks, including the Neptune Fountain, the Pedro de Valdivia Statue, and the Fort Hidalgo. The structures are a blend of neoclassical, rococo, and Moorish styles, adding a touch of grandeur and charm to the hill's natural beauty.

Gardens and Landscapes

The hill is adorned with meticulously maintained gardens and green spaces that create a peaceful and serene atmosphere. As you ascend the winding pathways, you'll encounter lush vegetation, colorful flowers, and picturesque nooks that invite contemplation and relaxation. The gardens are dotted with benches and shaded areas, providing ideal spots to unwind and enjoy the tranquil surroundings.

Panoramic Views

One of the highlights of visiting Santa Lucía Hill is the panoramic view it offers of Santiago. Once you reach the top, you're rewarded with a breathtaking vista that stretches across the cityscape, encompassing iconic landmarks, such as the Andes Mountains, the Mapocho River, and the modern skyline of Santiago. The view is particularly enchanting at sunset when the sky transforms into a palette of vibrant colors.

Cultural Significance

Santa Lucía Hill has significant cultural value as it has been immortalized in literature and poetry. It is believed to have inspired the renowned Chilean poet Pablo Neruda, who wrote about the hill's allure and its influence on his artistic expression. The hill's tranquil setting and its ability to inspire creativity make it an integral part of Santiago's cultural heritage.

Leisure and Recreation

In addition to its historical and cultural significance, Santa Lucía Hill offers opportunities for leisure and recreation. Visitors can enjoy leisurely walks, picnics, or simply find a quiet spot to read a book or admire the views. The hill is also a popular spot for photography enthusiasts, who can capture the natural beauty and architectural details from various angles.

Santa Lucía Hill encapsulates the essence of Santiago, combining historical significance, architectural beauty, and natural splendor. Whether you're exploring the hill's historical landmarks, admiring the well-tended gardens, or marveling at the panoramic views, a visit to Santa Lucía Hill offers a memorable experience that allows you to connect with Santiago's past and present in a serene and picturesque setting.

Practical Information

Location: Santa Lucía Hill is located in the heart of Santiago, Chile. It is bordered by the Plaza de Armas to the north, the Palacio de La Moneda to the west, and the Barrio Lastarria to the south.

Opening Hours: Santa Lucía Hill is open to the public 24 hours a day, 7 days a week. However, the tourist office is open from 9:00 AM to 5:00 PM, 7 days a week.

Admission Fees: There is no admission fee to visit Santa Lucía Hill. However, there is a small fee to enter the tourist office and the museum.

Accessibility: Santa Lucía Hill is wheelchair accessible. There are ramps and elevators to all of the major attractions on the hill.

Facilities and Amenities: Santa Lucía Hill has a number of facilities and amenities, including:

- A tourist office
- A museum
- A number of restaurants
- A number of cafes
- A number of souvenir shops

- A number of benches and chairs where you can relax and enjoy the view

Guided Tours: There are a number of guided tours that are available for Santa Lucía Hill. These tours can be a great way to learn more about the history and culture of the hill.

Safety Guidelines: Santa Lucía Hill is a safe place to visit. However, it is always important to be aware of your surroundings and take precautions against petty theft.

Nearby Services: There are a number of nearby services available, including:

- Banks
- ATMs
- Restaurants
- Cafes
- Shops
- Hotels
- Hostels

Best Time to Visit: The best time to visit Santa Lucía Hill is during the day, when the sun is shining and the hill is bustling with activity. However, Santa Lucía Hill is also a beautiful place to visit at night, when the lights are turned on and the city views are spectacular.

Contact Information: If you need more information about Santa Lucía Hill, you can contact the tourist office at the following number:

+56 2 263 08 66

Here are some insider tips for visiting Santa Lucía Hill:

- Wear comfortable shoes, as there is a lot of walking involved.
- Bring sunscreen, as the hill can get very hot in the sun.
- Bring a water bottle, as it can be very dry in the sun.
- Allow at least 2 hours to explore Santa Lucía Hill.
- Take a guided tour to learn more about the history and culture of the hill.
- Visit the museum to learn more about the history of Santa Lucía Hill.
- Enjoy the views from the top of the hill, which offer stunning panoramic views of Santiago.
- Have lunch or dinner at one of the restaurants on the hill.
- Take a walk through the gardens and enjoy the lush vegetation.
- Visit the souvenir shops to find a unique memento of your visit to Santa Lucía Hill.

Metropolitan Cathedral

The Metropolitan Cathedral, situated in the heart of Santiago, Chile, is a majestic and significant religious landmark that embodies the city's deep-rooted spirituality and rich cultural heritage. As the seat of the Archdiocese of Santiago, the cathedral holds immense religious importance for Catholics in

Chile and attracts visitors from around the world. Here, we explore the unique features and cultural significance of the Metropolitan Cathedral.

Historical Heritage

The Metropolitan Cathedral boasts a long and storied history that dates back to the 16th century. Construction of the original cathedral began in 1561 under the direction of the Spanish conquistador Pedro de Valdivia. Over the centuries, the cathedral has undergone various renovations and expansions, resulting in a blend of architectural styles, including neoclassical and neo-Renaissance elements. As you approach the cathedral, its impressive façade and grand scale evoke a sense of awe and reverence.

Architectural Splendor

The Metropolitan Cathedral's architectural beauty is a testament to the craftsmanship of skilled artisans over the centuries. The cathedral features intricately carved facades, towering columns, and graceful arches that exemplify the neoclassical and neo-Renaissance styles. The interior is adorned with exquisite religious artwork, including paintings, sculptures, and religious artifacts that reflect the spiritual devotion of Chile's Catholic community.

Chapel of the Blessed Sacrament

One of the most revered areas within the cathedral is the Chapel of the Blessed Sacrament. This sacred space is a place of contemplation and prayer, adorned with ornate altars, stained glass windows, and religious iconography. The chapel's serene atmosphere invites visitors to reflect and find solace in the tranquility of their surroundings.

The Tomb of Bernardo O'Higgins

The Metropolitan Cathedral houses the final resting place of Bernardo O'Higgins, one of Chile's founding fathers and a key figure in the country's struggle for independence. The tomb of O'Higgins is a revered national monument and serves as a reminder of his significant contributions to Chile's history and identity.

Religious Ceremonies and Events

The Metropolitan Cathedral plays a pivotal role in the religious life of Santiago. It is a site of frequent religious ceremonies, including Masses, baptisms, weddings, and special religious observances. The cathedral's grand interior provides an awe-inspiring backdrop for these events, elevating the sense of spiritual significance and sacredness.

Cultural and Tourist Attraction

Beyond its religious importance, the Metropolitan Cathedral is a significant cultural and tourist attraction. Visitors from around the world come to admire the cathedral's architectural magnificence, explore its historical heritage, and experience the spiritual ambiance within its walls. The cathedral's central location in Santiago also makes it a prominent landmark that is easily accessible to locals and tourists alike.

The Metropolitan Cathedral stands as a testament to Santiago's profound religious devotion and cultural heritage. Whether you are a devout Catholic seeking spiritual solace or a traveler with an appreciation for historical and architectural marvels, a visit to the Metropolitan Cathedral promises an enriching and soul-stirring experience that captures the essence of Santiago's spiritual and cultural essence.

Practical Information

Location: The Metropolitan Cathedral is located in the heart of Santiago, Chile. It is on the north side of Plaza de Armas.

Opening Hours: The Metropolitan Cathedral is open to the public from 8:30 AM to 8:00 PM, 7 days a week.

Admission Fees: There is no admission fee to visit the Metropolitan Cathedral.

Accessibility: The Metropolitan Cathedral is wheelchair accessible. There is a ramp leading up to the main entrance, and there are elevators to the upper levels of the cathedral.

Facilities and Amenities: The Metropolitan Cathedral has a number of facilities and amenities, including:

- A gift shop
- A bookstore
- A cafe
- A restroom

Guided Tours: There are a number of guided tours that are available for the Metropolitan Cathedral. These tours can be a great way to learn more about the history and architecture of the cathedral.

Safety Guidelines: The Metropolitan Cathedral is a safe place to visit. However, it is always important to be aware of your surroundings and take precautions against petty theft.

Nearby Services: There are a number of nearby services available, including:

- Banks
- ATMs
- Restaurants
- Cafes
- Shops
- Hotels
- Hostels

Best Time to Visit: The best time to visit the Metropolitan Cathedral is during the day, when the sun is shining and the cathedral is in full view. However, the cathedral is also a beautiful place to visit at night, when it is illuminated.

Contact Information: If you need more information about the Metropolitan Cathedral, you can contact the cathedral office at the following number:

+56 2 263 08 44

Here are some insider tips for visiting the Metropolitan Cathedral:

- Wear comfortable shoes, as there is a lot of walking involved.
- Bring sunscreen, as the cathedral can get very hot in the sun.
- Bring a water bottle, as it can be very dry in the sun.
- Allow at least 30 minutes to explore the cathedral.

- Take a guided tour to learn more about the history and architecture of the cathedral.
- Visit the gift shop to purchase souvenirs of your visit.
- Visit the bookstore to purchase books about the history of Chile and Santiago.
- Have lunch or dinner at one of the restaurants near the cathedral.
- Take a walk through Plaza de Armas and enjoy the lively atmosphere.
- Visit the other historical buildings in the area, such as the Palacio de La Moneda and the Palacio de los Tribunales.

Bellavista Neighborhood

Nestled at the base of San Cristóbal Hill, Bellavista is a vibrant and bohemian neighborhood in Santiago, Chile. Known for its artistic flair, colorful streets, and lively atmosphere, Bellavista has earned a reputation as one of the city's most captivating and eclectic districts. Here, we explore the unique features and cultural significance of the Bellavista neighborhood.

Artistic and Bohemian Vibes

Bellavista is a haven for artists, creatives, and free spirits, creating an unmistakable bohemian ambiance. The neighborhood's streets are adorned with vibrant murals, street art, and graffiti, adding to its artistic allure. Art galleries, independent boutiques, and craft shops dot the area, showcasing the work of local artists and artisans. Bellavista's artistic soul resonates through its colorful facades and creative energy.

Pablo Neruda's La Chascona

One of the most notable attractions in Bellavista is La Chascona, the former residence of Chilean poet Pablo Neruda. This unique house-museum is a must-visit, offering a glimpse into Neruda's life and poetic inspiration. La Chascona's quirky architecture, charming gardens, and breathtaking views of the city provide a poetic experience that captivates visitors.

Cultural Hotspot

Bellavista is a cultural hotspot that comes alive with theater performances, live music, and cultural events. The neighborhood is home to several theaters, including Teatro La Feria and Teatro Universidad de Chile, which host an array of performances, from contemporary theater to live music concerts. Bellavista's nightlife is equally vibrant, with numerous bars, clubs, and live music venues, ensuring that the energy and excitement continue long into the night.

Gastronomic Delights

Food enthusiasts will find plenty to delight in Bellavista, as the neighborhood offers a diverse culinary scene. From traditional Chilean dishes to international cuisine, the area's restaurants, cafés, and food stalls cater to all tastes. Bellavista's bustling Pío Nono street is particularly famous for its street food and local delicacies, making it an ideal spot to savor authentic Chilean flavors.

Cerro San Cristóbal

Bellavista's proximity to Cerro San Cristóbal, a prominent hill that towers over Santiago, adds to its allure. The hill offers hiking trails, beautiful viewpoints, and the iconic Virgen de la Inmaculada Concepción statue, which stands tall atop the hill. A visit to Cerro San Cristóbal provides a chance to escape the city's hustle and bustle and immerse oneself in nature's serenity.

Centenario Pool

Another beloved landmark in Bellavista is the Centenario Pool, a historic outdoor swimming pool that has been part of the neighborhood since 1928. The pool's Art Deco design and inviting waters make it a popular spot to cool off during Santiago's warm summers.

Bellavista's eclectic charm, artistic spirit, and cultural vibrancy make it a must-visit destination for those exploring Santiago. Whether you're wandering through its colorful streets, soaking in the poetry of La Chascona, indulging in delicious cuisine, or embracing the artistic energy that permeates the neighborhood, Bellavista promises an unforgettable experience that captures the heart and soul of Santiago's bohemian spirit.

Practical Information

Location: Bellavista is located in the heart of Santiago, Chile. It is bordered by the Mapocho River to the east, the Cerro San Cristóbal to the west, and the Parque Forestal to the south.

Opening Hours: Bellavista is open to the public 24 hours a day, 7 days a week. However, the shops and restaurants in the neighborhood are open during regular business hours.

Admission Fees: There is no admission fee to visit Bellavista.

Accessibility: Bellavista is a relatively accessible neighborhood. There are ramps and elevators in most of the buildings, and the streets are wide enough for wheelchairs.

Facilities and Amenities: Bellavista has a number of facilities and amenities, including:

- A variety of restaurants

- A variety of shops
- A number of bars
- A number of art galleries
- A number of theaters
- A number of parks

Guided Tours: There are a number of guided tours that are available for Bellavista. These tours can be a great way to learn more about the history and culture of the neighborhood.

Safety Guidelines: Bellavista is a safe neighborhood. However, it is always important to be aware of your surroundings and take precautions against petty theft.

Nearby Services: There are a number of nearby services available, including:

- Banks
- ATMs
- Restaurants
- Cafes
- Shops
- Hotels
- Hostels

Best Time to Visit: The best time to visit Bellavista is during the day, when the sun is shining and the neighborhood is in full view. The neighborhood is also lively at night, as many of the bars and restaurants stay open late.

Contact Information: If you need more information about Bellavista, you can contact the Santiago Tourism office at the following number:

+56 2 29412000

Here are some insider tips for visiting Bellavista:

- Wear comfortable shoes, as there is a lot of walking involved.
- Bring sunscreen, as the neighborhood can get very hot in the sun.
- Bring a water bottle, as it can be very dry in the sun.
- Allow at least 3 hours to explore Bellavista.
- Visit the restaurants and bars to sample the local cuisine.
- Visit the art galleries and theaters to experience the local arts scene.
- Take a walk through the parks to relax and enjoy the scenery.

Santiago Metropolitan Park

Santiago Metropolitan Park, also known as Parque Metropolitano de Santiago, is a vast urban oasis and one of the largest urban parks in the world. Nestled amidst the bustling city, this expansive green space offers residents and visitors alike a refreshing escape into nature and a wide range of recreational activities. Here, we delve into the unique features and natural beauty of Santiago Metropolitan Park.

Spectacular Location

Santiago Metropolitan Park is strategically located on the slopes of San Cristóbal Hill, which rises majestically above the city. The park's elevated position provides breathtaking panoramic views of Santiago's skyline, the surrounding mountains, and the Andes in the distance. The park's lush greenery juxtaposed against the urban landscape creates a stunning visual contrast.

Biodiversity and Wildlife

The park is home to a diverse array of flora and fauna, making it a haven for nature enthusiasts and wildlife lovers. Numerous tree species, including eucalyptus and cypress, dot the landscape, creating shaded areas perfect for picnics and relaxation. Visitors may also encounter native bird species, such as the Chilean tinamou and the Chilean mockingbird, as well as small mammals like rabbits and foxes.

Cerro San Cristóbal

At the heart of Santiago Metropolitan Park lies Cerro San Cristóbal, a prominent hill that offers several hiking trails and roadways leading to its summit. Visitors can choose to hike, bike, or drive to the top, where they will be rewarded with unparalleled views of Santiago and its surroundings. The hilltop is also home to the iconic Virgin Mary statue, known as Virgen de la Inmaculada Concepción, which has become an emblematic symbol of the city.

Recreation and Leisure

The park provides an extensive range of recreational activities to cater to all ages and interests. Families can enjoy picnics, play areas, and playgrounds scattered throughout the park. Fitness enthusiasts can take advantage of the various jogging and cycling paths, as well as outdoor gyms. Additionally, there are picnic spots, barbecue areas, and designated spaces for outdoor gatherings and events.

Santiago Metropolitan Zoo

Nestled within the park is the Santiago Metropolitan Zoo, a popular attraction for visitors of all ages. The zoo houses a diverse collection of animals from different continents, providing educational and enriching experiences for visitors. The zoo's conservation efforts and focus on animal welfare make it an important institution for promoting wildlife preservation and awareness.

Teleférico and Funicular

For a unique way to explore the park, visitors can use the Teleférico (cable car) or the Funicular railway. The Teleférico offers an aerial journey that glides above the trees, providing magnificent views of the park and the city. The Funicular, on the other hand, ascends the hill in a historic railway carriage, offering a nostalgic and charming experience.

Santiago Metropolitan Park is more than just a recreational space; it is an essential part of Santiago's identity and a cherished escape for its residents. With its natural beauty, recreational opportunities, and sweeping views, the park offers a perfect blend of nature and urban living, inviting all to unwind, connect with nature, and experience the spirit of Santiago.

Practical Information

Location: Santiago Metropolitan Park is located in the east of Santiago, Chile. It is bordered by the Mapocho River to the north, the Cerro Santa Lucía to the west, and the Parque Forestal to the south.

Opening Hours: Monday to Friday, 6:30 AM-9:00 PM.

Admission Fees: There is no admission fee to visit Santiago Metropolitan Park.

Accessibility: Santiago Metropolitan Park is wheelchair accessible. There are ramps and elevators throughout the park, and the paths are wide enough for wheelchairs.

Facilities and Amenities: Santiago Metropolitan Park has a number of facilities and amenities, including:

- A variety of restaurants
- A variety of shops
- A number of ponds
- A number of hiking trails
- A number of playgrounds
- A number of picnic areas

Guided Tours: There are a number of guided tours that are available for Santiago Metropolitan Park. These tours can be a great way to learn more about the history and culture of the park.

Safety Guidelines: Santiago Metropolitan Park is a safe park. However, it is always important to be aware of your surroundings and take precautions against petty theft.

Nearby Services: There are a number of nearby services available, including:

- Banks
- ATMs
- Restaurants
- Cafes
- Shops

- Hotels
- Hostels

Best Time to Visit: The best time to visit Santiago Metropolitan Park is during the day, when the sun is shining and the park is in full view. The park is also lively at night, as many of the restaurants and bars stay open late.

Contact Information: If you need more information about Santiago Metropolitan Park, you can contact the Santiago Tourism office at the following number:

+56 2 29412000

Here are some insider tips for visiting Santiago Metropolitan Park:

- Wear comfortable shoes, as there is a lot of walking involved.
- Bring sunscreen, as the park can get very hot in the sun.
- Bring a water bottle, as it can be very dry in the sun.
- Allow at least 3 hours to explore Santiago Metropolitan Park.
- Visit the restaurants and bars to sample the local cuisine.
- Visit the ponds and hiking trails to enjoy the natural beauty of the park.
- Take the kids to the playgrounds and picnic areas to let them run around and play.

Museums and Cultural Sites

Chilean Museum of Pre-Columbian Art

The Chilean Museum of Pre-Columbian Art is a captivating cultural institution .that showcases the rich and diverse heritage of the indigenous peoples of the Americas. With an extensive collection of pre-Columbian artifacts, the museum offers a fascinating journey through the history and artistic achievements of the region's ancient civilizations. Here, we explore the unique features and cultural significance of the Chilean Museum of Pre-Columbian Art.

Historical Heritage

The museum is housed in the former Royal Customs House, a neoclassical building that dates back to the 19th century. Its architecture adds to the museum's allure, providing a fitting backdrop for the ancient treasures it houses. The museum was established in 1981, and since then, it has become a valuable repository of pre-Columbian art and culture.

Vast Collection of Artifacts

The Chilean Museum of Pre-Columbian Art boasts an impressive and diverse collection of over 3,000 artifacts from various pre-Columbian cultures throughout the Americas. The exhibits span over 4,500 years of history, showcasing artifacts from the indigenous civilizations of Chile, Peru, Ecuador, Colombia, Mexico, and beyond. Visitors can explore intricate pottery, textiles, ceramics, metalwork, and stone carvings that represent the artistic achievements and cultural practices of these ancient societies.

Themed Galleries

The museum's collection is organized into themed galleries, providing a structured and immersive experience for visitors. Each gallery focuses on specific aspects of pre-Columbian life, such as religious beliefs, social structures, and artistic expressions. Through carefully curated displays and informative exhibits, visitors gain insights into the daily lives and spiritual beliefs of the indigenous peoples of the Americas.

Cultural and Educational Significance

The Chilean Museum of Pre-Columbian Art holds immense cultural and educational significance. It serves as an important platform for preserving and promoting the cultural heritage of pre-Columbian civilizations, fostering an appreciation for their artistic achievements and contributions to human history. The museum also plays a vital role in educating visitors about the diverse and complex cultures that thrived in the Americas before the arrival of Europeans.

Temporary Exhibitions and Events

In addition to its permanent collection, the museum regularly hosts temporary exhibitions that delve into specific aspects of pre-Columbian art and history. These special exhibits offer fresh perspectives and further enrich the museum experience. Furthermore, the museum organizes educational programs, workshops, and lectures to engage visitors and deepen their understanding of pre-Columbian cultures.

Cultural Exchange

The Chilean Museum of Pre-Columbian Art actively engages in cultural exchange programs with other museums and institutions worldwide. These collaborations facilitate the sharing of knowledge and artifacts, contributing to a broader understanding of pre-Columbian cultures on an international scale.

The Chilean Museum of Pre-Columbian Art stands as a testament to the rich legacy of the Americas' indigenous peoples. Through its diverse collection and engaging exhibitions, it provides a bridge between the ancient past and the present, offering visitors a unique opportunity to connect with the art, history, and cultural heritage of the pre-Columbian world. The museum's commitment to preservation, education, and cultural exchange ensures that the legacy of these ancient civilizations continues to inspire and captivate generations to come.

Practical Information

Location: The Chilean Museum of Pre-Columbian Art is located in the heart of Santiago, Chile. It is on the block of Bandera 361, between Morandé and Agustinas, in the Centro Historico neighborhood.

Opening Hours: The museum is open Tuesday through Friday from 10:00 AM to 6:00 PM, and on Saturday and Sunday from 11:00 AM to 7:00 PM.

Admission Fees: The entrance fee for adults is $5,000 CLP (about $7 USD). There a discounted rate of $3,000 CLP (about $4 USD) for students, seniors, and people with disabilities. Children under 12 are free.

Accessibility: The museum is wheelchair accessible. There is a ramp leading up to the main entrance, and there are elevators throughout the museum.

Facilities and Amenities: The museum has a number of facilities and amenities, including:

- A gift shop
- A cafe
- A restroom
- A library

Guided Tours: There are a number of guided tours that are available for the Chilean Museum of Pre-Columbian Art. These tours can be a great way to learn more about the history and culture of the artifacts on display.

Safety Guidelines: The museum is a safe place to visit. However, it is always important to be aware of your surroundings and take precautions against petty theft.

Nearby Services: There are a number of nearby services available, including:

- Banks
- ATMs
- Restaurants
- Cafes
- Shops
- Hotels
- Hostels

Best Time to Visit: The best time to visit the Chilean Museum of Pre-Columbian Art is during the day, when the museum is open and the artifacts are on display. The museum is also lively at night, as many of the restaurants and bars stay open late.

Contact Information: If you need more information about the Chilean Museum of Pre-Columbian Art, you can contact the museum at the following number:

+56 2 233 0180

Here are some insider tips for visiting the Chilean Museum of Pre-Columbian Art:

- Wear comfortable shoes, as there is a lot of walking involved.
- Bring sunscreen, as the museum can get very hot in the sun.
- Bring a water bottle, as it can be very dry in the sun.
- Allow at least 2 hours to explore the museum.
- Take a guided tour to learn more about the history and culture of the artifacts on display.
- Visit the gift shop to purchase souvenirs of your visit.
- Visit the cafe to enjoy a cup of coffee or a snack.
- Visit the library to learn more about the history of pre-Columbian art.

Museum of Memory and Human Rights

The Museum of Memory and Human Rights is a poignant and deeply significant institution dedicated to preserving the memory of the country's turbulent past and advocating for human rights. Established in 2010, the museum serves as a powerful testament to the victims of human rights abuses during Chile's dark period of dictatorship. Here, we explore the unique features and cultural significance of the Museum of Memory and Human Rights.

Historical Context

The Museum of Memory and Human Rights was established to commemorate and honor the victims of human rights violations that occurred during the military dictatorship of Augusto Pinochet (1973-1990). During this period, Chile experienced widespread repression, torture, disappearances, and other grave human rights abuses. The museum's mission is to ensure that this painful chapter of history is never forgotten, fostering a collective understanding and commitment to human rights.

Architectural Symbolism

The museum's architecture and design hold deep symbolism. The building's exterior features a striking facade with copper plates that represent the "missing" and "detained" individuals during the dictatorship. The architecture is a poignant reminder of the loss and suffering endured by countless Chileans during that era. Inside, the museum's layout and exhibits are carefully curated to create an emotional and immersive experience for visitors.

Thematic Exhibitions

The Museum of Memory and Human Rights features thematic exhibitions that shed light on different aspects of the dictatorship and its impact on Chilean society. The exhibits include historical photographs, personal testimonies, archival documents, and audiovisual materials that provide a comprehensive and moving narrative of the era. The museum aims to confront the painful past while promoting a culture of human rights and social justice.

Tribute to the Victims

One of the museum's central objectives is to pay tribute to the victims and survivors of human rights abuses. Through audio recordings, personal accounts, and interactive exhibits, the museum humanizes the victims and gives them a voice, ensuring that their stories are preserved for future generations. By doing so, the museum serves as a place of healing and remembrance for families who lost loved ones during those dark years.

Educational Initiatives

The Museum of Memory and Human Rights is dedicated to education and outreach. It offers educational programs for students, workshops, and seminars on human rights, democracy, and social justice. By engaging with young generations, the museum fosters critical thinking and empathy, encouraging a collective commitment to human rights and the prevention of atrocities in the future.

Advocacy for Human Rights

In addition to its role as a memorial and educational center, the museum actively advocates for human rights in Chile and beyond. It collaborates with other human rights organizations, both nationally and internationally, to promote accountability for past atrocities and advocate for justice and human rights protection.

The Museum of Memory and Human Rights stands as a testament to Chile's commitment to never forget the horrors of the past and to promote a society built on respect for human dignity and social justice. Through its powerful exhibits and educational initiatives, the museum challenges visitors to confront the legacy of human rights abuses and to actively work towards a future where human rights are upheld and protected for all. It serves as a solemn reminder that remembering and acknowledging the past is essential to building a more just and compassionate society.

Practical Information

Location: The Museum of Memory and Human Rights is located in the heart of Santiago, Chile. It is on the block of Matucana 501, between Catedral and San Diego, in the Barrio Lastarria neighborhood.

Opening Hours: The museum is open Tuesday through Friday from 10:00 AM to 6:00 PM, and on Saturday and Sunday from 11:00 AM to 7:00 PM.

Admission Fees: The entrance fee for adults is $5,000 CLP (about $7 USD). There is a discounted rate of $3,000 CLP (about $4 USD) for students, seniors, and people with disabilities. Children under 12 are free.

Accessibility: The museum is wheelchair accessible. There is a ramp leading up to the main entrance, and there are elevators throughout the museum.

Facilities and Amenities: The museum has a number of facilities and amenities, including:

- A gift shop
- A cafe
- A restroom
- A library

Guided Tours: The museum offers guided tours in Spanish and English. Tours are available Tuesday through Friday at 11:00 AM and 3:00 PM, and on Saturday and Sunday at 11:00 AM, 1:00 PM, and 3:00 PM.

Safety Guidelines: The museum is a safe place to visit. However, it is always important to be aware of your surroundings and take precautions against petty theft.

Nearby Services: There are a number of nearby services available, including:

- Banks
- ATMs
- Restaurants
- Cafes
- Shops
- Hotels
- Hostels

Best Time to Visit: The best time to visit the Museum of Memory and Human Rights is during the day, when the museum is open and the exhibits are available to be viewed. The museum is also lively at night, as many of the restaurants and bars stay open late.

Contact Information: If you need more information about the Museum of Memory and Human Rights, you can contact the museum at the following number:

+56 2 2597 9600

Here are some insider tips for visiting the Museum of Memory and Human Rights:

- Allow at least 2 hours to explore the museum.
- Take a guided tour to learn more about the history of human rights abuses in Chile.
- Visit the exhibit on the 1973 coup d'état.
- Visit the exhibit on the Pinochet dictatorship.
- Visit the exhibit on the fight for human rights in Chile.
- Visit the library to learn more about the history of human rights in Chile.

Museum of Fine Arts

The Museum of Fine Arts is a cultural treasure that showcases an extensive and diverse collection of artwork spanning various artistic movements and periods. As one of the oldest and most prestigious art museums in Latin America, the institution is dedicated to promoting the appreciation of visual arts and providing visitors with enriching experiences. Here, we explore the unique features and cultural significance of the Museum of Fine Arts.

Historical Legacy

The Museum of Fine Arts was founded in 1880, making it one of the oldest museums in Chile. Its establishment was a testament to Chile's growing cultural appreciation and desire to nurture the arts. Throughout its long history, the museum has evolved, expanded, and adapted to become the esteemed institution it is today.

Extensive Art Collection

The museum's collection boasts an impressive array of artwork, covering diverse genres, artistic styles, and time periods. Visitors can admire works by renowned Chilean artists, such as Roberto

Matta and Claudio Bravo, as well as prominent international artists like Vincent van Gogh, Auguste Rodin, and Claude Monet. The collection includes paintings, sculptures, prints, drawings, photographs, and decorative arts, providing a comprehensive representation of art history.

Thematic Exhibitions

The Museum of Fine Arts hosts temporary exhibitions and thematic displays that explore specific aspects of art and artists. These exhibitions often focus on particular artistic movements, historical periods, or cultural themes, allowing visitors to delve deeper into the context and significance of the artworks. The museum's dynamic program ensures a continuous flow of new and engaging content for visitors to explore.

Promoting Chilean Art

The museum plays a vital role in promoting and supporting Chilean artists and their work. It provides a platform for emerging talents to showcase their art, fostering a vibrant and diverse artistic community. By showcasing Chilean art alongside international masterpieces, the museum encourages dialogue and cross-cultural exchange, enriching the artistic landscape of Chile.

Educational Programs

The Museum of Fine Arts is committed to education and offers various programs and activities for all ages. Guided tours, workshops, lectures, and educational materials cater to students, families, and art enthusiasts. These initiatives aim to cultivate a deeper understanding and appreciation of art, nurturing creativity and fostering a lifelong love for the arts.

Cultural Center

Beyond its role as a museum, the institution serves as a cultural center that hosts concerts, film screenings, literary events, and other cultural activities. This multidisciplinary approach encourages the integration of different artistic expressions, creating a vibrant cultural hub that attracts a diverse audience.

The Museum of Fine Arts stands as a testament to Chile's appreciation for the arts and its commitment to preserving and promoting cultural heritage. Through its extensive collection, thematic exhibitions, educational initiatives, and support for local artists, the museum provides a window into the world of art, inspiring and enriching the lives of its visitors. As a cultural gem in Santiago, the Museum of Fine Arts invites all to immerse themselves in the beauty, creativity, and richness of the visual arts.

Practical Information

Location: The Museum of Fine Arts is located in the heart of Santiago, Chile. It is on the block of José Miguel de la Barra 650, between Monjitas and Merced, in the Centro Historico neighborhood.

Opening Hours: The museum is open Tuesday through Sunday from 10:00 AM to 6:00 PM.

Admission Fees: The entrance fee for adults is $6,000 CLP (about $8 USD). There is a discounted rate of $4,000 CLP (about $6 USD) for students, seniors, and people with disabilities. Children under 6 are free.

Accessibility: The museum is wheelchair accessible. There is a ramp leading up to the main entrance, and there are elevators throughout the museum.

Facilities and Amenities: The museum has a number of facilities and amenities, including:

- A gift shop
- A cafe
- A restroom
- A library

Guided Tours: The museum offers guided tours in Spanish and English. Tours are available Tuesday through Sunday at 11:00 AM, 1:00 PM, and 3:00 PM.

Safety Guidelines: The museum is a safe place to visit. However, it is always important to be aware of your surroundings and take precautions against petty theft.

Nearby Services: There are a number of nearby services available, including:

- Banks

- ATMs
- Restaurants
- Cafes
- Shops
- Hotels
- Hostels

Best Time to Visit: The best time to visit the Museum of Fine Arts is during the day, when the museum is open and the exhibits are available to be viewed. The museum can be crowded on weekends.

Contact Information: If you need more information about the Museum of Fine Arts, you can contact the museum at the following number:

+56 2 2997 8700

Here are some insider tips for visiting the Museum of Fine Arts:

- Allow at least 3 hours to explore the museum.
- Take a guided tour to learn more about the history of the museum and the art on display.
- Visit the permanent collection, which includes works by Pablo Picasso, Salvador Dali, and Vincent van Gogh.
- Visit the temporary exhibitions, which feature a variety of art from around the world.
- Visit the library to learn more about art history and the museum's collection.

- Have lunch or dinner at one of the restaurants near the museum.
- Take a walk through the Centro Historico neighborhood to see other historical buildings and attractions.

Outdoor Activities and Day Trips

Wine Tasting in the Maipo Valley

Nestled amidst the picturesque Andes Mountains and lush vineyards, the Maipo Valley in Chile offers a delightful and unforgettable wine tasting experience. As one of the country's most renowned wine regions, the Maipo Valley is celebrated for its exceptional wines and breathtaking landscapes. Here, we delve into the unique features and cultural significance of wine tasting in the Maipo Valley.

A Wine Lover's Paradise

The Maipo Valley is a true paradise for wine enthusiasts and connoisseurs. With its ideal climate, fertile soils, and rich winemaking traditions, the valley has earned its reputation as one of Chile's premier wine-producing regions. Renowned for its Cabernet Sauvignon, the valley's vineyards also yield exceptional Merlot, Syrah, and Carmenere wines, among others.

Historic Wineries

The Maipo Valley is home to some of Chile's oldest and most iconic wineries, many of which have been in operation for generations. These historic wineries not only offer exquisite wines but also provide a glimpse into the country's winemaking heritage and the passion that goes into crafting each bottle.

Vineyard Tours

Wine tasting in the Maipo Valley is often accompanied by guided vineyard tours. Visitors have the opportunity to explore the sprawling vineyards, where they can learn about the winemaking process, from grape cultivation to fermentation and aging. This immersive experience offers a deeper understanding of the dedication and craftsmanship that goes into producing each vintage.

Wine Cellar Visits

Many wineries in the Maipo Valley boast impressive wine cellars that house barrels of aging wines. These atmospheric cellars provide the perfect setting for wine tastings, allowing visitors to sample a variety of vintages and discover the unique characteristics imparted by time and oak.

Wine and Gastronomy

Wine tasting in the Maipo Valley is often complemented by exceptional gastronomic experiences. Many wineries have on-site restaurants that pair their wines with delectable dishes crafted from locally sourced ingredients. The fusion of exquisite wines and gourmet cuisine creates a feast for the senses, enhancing the overall tasting experience.

Majestic Scenery

Beyond the pleasure of wine tasting, the Maipo Valley's stunning scenery adds an extra dimension to the journey.

Surrounded by the grandeur of the Andes Mountains, the vineyards and wineries in the valley offer breathtaking views that provide a serene and picturesque backdrop for the wine tasting experience.

Wine Festivals and Events

Throughout the year, the Maipo Valley hosts various wine festivals and events that celebrate the region's winemaking culture. These events offer a chance to taste wines from different wineries, attend seminars, and immerse oneself in the convivial atmosphere of wine lovers from around the world.

Wine tasting in the Maipo Valley is not just a sensory delight; it's a celebration of Chile's winemaking heritage and a journey into the passion and dedication of its wine producers. As you savor each sip and embrace the stunning surroundings, you'll find yourself enchanted by the magic of the Maipo Valley, making your wine tasting experience a memorable and enriching adventure.

Here are some insider tips for enjoying wine tasting in the Maipo Valley:

- **Choose the right time of year.** The best time to go wine tasting in the Maipo Valley is during the spring (September-November) or fall (March-May). The weather is mild during these months, and the grapes are at their peak ripeness.

- **Book your visit in advance.** Many wineries are popular, and it's best to book your visit in advance to avoid disappointment.
- **Wear comfortable shoes.** You'll be doing a lot of walking, so make sure to wear comfortable shoes.
- **Bring sunscreen and a hat.** The weather in the Maipo Valley can be hot, so it's important to protect yourself from the sun.
- **Drink plenty of water.** Wine tasting can dehydrate you, so it's important to drink plenty of water.
- **Start with white wines.** White wines are lighter and easier to drink than red wines. It's a good idea to start with white wines and then move on to red wines.
- **Pair your wines with food.** Wine is meant to be enjoyed with food. Pairing your wines with food can help you to appreciate the flavors of the wine.
- **Don't be afraid to ask questions.** The winemakers at the wineries are happy to answer your questions about the wines.

Here are some other additional tips:

- **Try a variety of wines.** The Maipo Valley is home to a wide variety of wines, so try a few different ones to see what you like.
- **Ask for recommendations.** The winemakers at the wineries are happy to recommend wines that you might enjoy.

- **Take your time.** There's no need to rush through your wine tasting. Enjoy the experience and take your time to savor the flavors of the wine.
- **Have fun!** Wine tasting is a great way to relax and enjoy the company of friends. Make sure to relax and have fun.

Cajón del Maipo

Nestled in the Andes Mountains, Cajón del Maipo is a breathtakingly beautiful and enchanting destination located just outside Santiago, Chile. This picturesque canyon is a haven for nature lovers and adventure seekers, offering a diverse range of outdoor activities and awe-inspiring landscapes. Here, we explore the unique features and cultural significance of Cajón del Maipo.

Natural Beauty

Cajón del Maipo is celebrated for its unparalleled natural beauty. The canyon is characterized by its towering mountains, pristine rivers, lush forests, and glistening glaciers. The Maipo River flows through the heart of the canyon, adding to the mesmerizing scenery and providing opportunities for various water-based activities.

Hiking and Trekking

For those seeking outdoor adventure, Cajón del Maipo is a paradise for hiking and trekking. The region offers an array of trails that cater to different skill levels, from leisurely walks to challenging mountain treks. As you venture along the trails, you'll be treated to stunning vistas of snow-capped peaks, cascading waterfalls, and verdant valleys.

Hot Springs

Cajón del Maipo is home to natural hot springs, which are a popular attraction for visitors seeking relaxation and rejuvenation. The soothing waters are surrounded by picturesque landscapes, providing a tranquil and therapeutic escape from the hustle and bustle of everyday life.

Adventure Sports

The canyon's rugged terrain makes it a playground for adventure sports enthusiasts. Rock climbing, rappelling, white-water rafting, and horseback riding are among the adrenaline-pumping activities that can be enjoyed in Cajón del Maipo. These activities allow you to immerse yourself in the region's natural wonders while experiencing an exhilarating sense of thrill.

Stargazing

Cajón del Maipo's remote location and clear skies make it an ideal spot for stargazing. Away from city lights, the canyon offers an unobstructed view of the night sky, allowing visitors to witness the celestial wonders above. Stargazing tours and observatories provide opportunities to learn about the constellations and astronomical phenomena that grace the southern skies.

Ecotourism and Sustainability

Cajón del Maipo is committed to ecotourism and sustainable practices to preserve its natural environment and cultural heritage. Local communities are actively involved in promoting responsible tourism, supporting the conservation of the canyon's unique ecosystems, and fostering an appreciation for its cultural significance.

Connection to Local Culture

The canyon is not only a natural wonder but also a place rich in cultural heritage. Indigenous communities have lived in the region for centuries and continue to preserve their traditions and customs. Visitors have the chance to learn about the ancient cultural practices and gain insights into the deep-rooted connections between the land and its people.

Cajón del Maipo offers a captivating escape into nature, where the magnificence of the Andes unfolds before your eyes. Whether you're seeking adventure, relaxation, or a chance to reconnect with nature and local culture, the canyon's allure will leave you spellbound and create cherished memories that last a lifetime.

Here are some insider tips for outdoor activities in Cajón del Maipo:

- **Hiking:** Cajón del Maipo is a great place for hiking. There are a variety of trails to choose from, ranging from easy to challenging. Some popular hiking trails include the following:
    - **Inca Trail:** This moderate trail is 10 kilometers long and takes about 4 hours to hike. It leads to the Inca ruins of Picarquín.
    - **Laguna del Morado:** This challenging trail is 15 kilometers long and takes about 6 hours to hike. It leads to the Morado Lagoon, which is a beautiful turquoise lake surrounded by snow-capped mountains.
    - **Cerro El Plomo:** This challenging trail is 22 kilometers long and takes about 10 hours to

hike. It leads to the summit of Cerro El Plomo, which is the second-highest mountain in Chile.

- **Mountain biking:** Cajón del Maipo is also a great place for mountain biking. There are a variety of trails to choose from, ranging from easy to challenging. Some popular mountain biking trails include the following:

  - **Laguna del Morado:** This moderate trail is 15 kilometers long and takes about 2 hours to bike. It leads to the Morado Lagoon, which is a beautiful turquoise lake surrounded by snow-capped mountains.

  - **Cerro El Plomo:** This challenging trail is 22 kilometers long and takes about 4 hours to bike. It leads to the summit of Cerro El Plomo, which is the second-highest mountain in Chile.

  - **Valle del Colorado:** This challenging trail is 15 kilometers long and takes about 3 hours to bike. It leads through the Colorado Valley, which is a beautiful desert valley with red sand dunes and rock formations.

- **Rafting:** Cajón del Maipo is also a great place for rafting. The Mapocho River is a popular spot for whitewater rafting, and there are a variety of rafting companies to choose from. Some popular rafting trips include the following:

- ○ **Class III:** This is a moderate rafting trip that is suitable for beginners and experienced rafters alike. It takes about 3 hours and includes a number of rapids.

- ○ **Class IV:** This is a challenging rafting trip that is only suitable for experienced rafters. It takes about 4 hours and includes a number of challenging rapids.

Here are some additional tips:

- **Check the weather conditions before you go.** The weather in Cajón del Maipo can change quickly, so it's important to check the weather conditions before you go.
- **Be prepared for anything.** The weather in Cajón del Maipo can be unpredictable, so it's important to be prepared for anything. Pack sunscreen, a hat, sunglasses, a raincoat, and extra clothes.
- **Let someone know where you're going.** Before you go on your outdoor adventure, let someone know where you're going and when you expect to be back. This is especially important if you're going on a solo hike or bike ride.
- **Be respectful of the environment.** Cajón del Maipo is a beautiful place, and it's important to be respectful of the environment. Pack out all of your trash and leave no trace of your visit.

- **Have fun!** Cajón del Maipo is a great place to get outdoors and enjoy the scenery. So relax, have fun, and enjoy your adventure.

Valparaíso and Viña del Mar

Valparaíso and Viña del Mar, two captivating cities on Chile's central coast, offer a delightful blend of rich cultural heritage, stunning landscapes, and vibrant coastal charm. Each city possesses its own distinct character and attractions, making them popular destinations for both local and international travelers. Let's explore the unique features and cultural significance of Valparaíso and Viña del Mar.

Valparaíso: A Bohemian Gem

Valparaíso, a UNESCO World Heritage Site, is a city renowned for its bohemian spirit, colorful architecture, and artistic vibe.

Perched on a series of steep hills overlooking the Pacific Ocean, Valparaíso's labyrinthine streets are adorned with eye-catching street art and vibrant murals, adding to its unique and bohemian ambiance. The city has long been a haven for artists, writers, and poets, who find inspiration in its artistic energy and lively cultural scene.

Cultural Richness

Valparaíso's cultural richness is evident in its numerous art galleries, theaters, and cultural centers. Visitors can explore the homes of famous poets like Pablo Neruda, who found solace and inspiration in the city's enchanting atmosphere. The city's vibrant nightlife and music scene add to its cultural allure, with live performances and concerts held in various venues.

Ascensores (Funiculars)

Valparaíso is famous for its ascensores, or funiculars, which are a unique and nostalgic way to traverse the city's hilly terrain. These century-old elevators transport locals and visitors up and down the hills, providing breathtaking views of the city and the picturesque harbor below.

Viña del Mar: The Garden City

In contrast to Valparaíso's bohemian charm, Viña del Mar is a modern and cosmopolitan city known for its pristine beaches, meticulously landscaped gardens, and upscale resorts. Often referred to as the "Garden City," Viña del Mar boasts numerous parks and green spaces that offer a peaceful respite from the bustling city life.

Exquisite Gardens

The city's most prominent gardens include the Quinta Vergara Park, home to the famous Viña del Mar International Song Festival, and the Flower Clock, an iconic floral clock that has become a symbol of the city. These well-maintained gardens add to the city's allure and create a serene atmosphere that beckons visitors to relax and unwind.

Coastal Beauty

Viña del Mar's stunning coastline stretches along the Pacific Ocean, offering miles of sandy beaches and scenic promenades. The city's inviting beaches are popular spots for sunbathing, water sports, and leisurely walks. The iconic "Fifth Region" Casino is another prominent landmark along the coast, adding a touch of glamour to the city's beachfront.

Festival and Events

Viña del Mar is also famous for hosting the annual Viña del Mar International Song Festival, a prestigious music event that attracts renowned artists from around the world. The festival showcases a diverse range of musical talents and draws music enthusiasts from all corners of the globe.

Harmony of Contrasts

The juxtaposition of Valparaíso's bohemian allure and Viña del Mar's modern charm creates a harmonious contrast that appeals to a diverse range of travelers. Whether it's exploring Valparaíso's art-filled streets, relishing Viña del Mar's seaside beauty, or immersing oneself in the cultural richness of both cities, a visit to Valparaíso and Viña del Mar promises a memorable and enriching experience that captures the essence of Chile's central coast.

Here is some practical information and insider tips for visiting Valparaíso and Viña del Mar as day trips from Santiago:

Location: Valparaíso and Viña del Mar are two coastal cities located about 120 kilometers (75 miles) west of Santiago.

Opening Hours: Valparaíso and Viña del Mar are both open 24 hours a day. However, most of the tourist attractions are open during regular business hours, which are usually from 10:00 AM to 6:00 PM.

Admission Fees: There are no admission fees to visit Valparaíso or Viña del Mar. However, there may be admission fees to visit some of the tourist attractions, such as the Cerro Concepción in Valparaíso or the Quinta Vergara Gardens in Viña del Mar.

Accessibility: Valparaíso and Viña del Mar are both relatively accessible cities. There are a number of elevators and ramps in both cities, and most of the tourist attractions are wheelchair accessible.

Facilities and Amenities: Both Valparaíso and Viña del Mar have a variety of facilities and amenities, including restaurants, cafes, shops, hotels, and hostels.

Valparaíso:

- **Best Time to Visit:** The best time to visit Valparaíso is during the spring (September-November) or fall (March-May). The weather is mild during these months, and the city is less crowded.
- **Insider Tips:**
  - **Take a walk through the historic quarter of Valparaíso.** The colorful houses and narrow streets are a sight to behold.

- ○ **Visit the Cerro Concepción.** This hill offers stunning views of the city and the port.
- ○ **Take a ride on the funicular.** This traditional mode of transportation is a great way to get around the city.
- ○ **Visit the Pablo Neruda Museum.** This museum is dedicated to the life and work of the Chilean poet.
- ○ **Enjoy the nightlife in Valparaíso.** The city has a vibrant nightlife scene, with a variety of bars and clubs to choose from.

Viña del Mar:

- • **Best Time to Visit:** The best time to visit Viña del Mar is during the summer (December-February). The weather is warm and sunny during these months, and the city is packed with tourists.
- • **Insider Tips:**
    - ○ **Take a walk along the beach.** The beaches in Viña del Mar are some of the best in Chile.
    - ○ **Visit the Quinta Vergara Gardens.** These beautiful gardens are home to a number of sculptures and fountains.
    - ○ **Attend the Viña del Mar International Song Festival.** This annual music festival is held in February and features a number of international artists.

o **Enjoy the nightlife in Viña del Mar.** The city has a vibrant nightlife scene, with a variety of bars and clubs to choose from.

Here are some additional tips for planning your day trip to Valparaíso and Viña del Mar:

- **Book your transportation in advance.** There are a number of companies that offer day trips to Valparaíso and Viña del Mar from Santiago. It's a good idea to book your transportation in advance, especially if you're traveling during peak season.

- **Pack sunscreen, a hat, and sunglasses.** The weather in Valparaíso and Viña del Mar can be hot and sunny, so it's important to pack sunscreen, a hat, and sunglasses.

- **Bring water.** It's important to stay hydrated, especially if you're planning on doing a lot of walking.

- **Dress comfortably.** You'll be doing a lot of walking, so it's a good idea to dress comfortably.

- **Allow enough time.** It's a good idea to allow at least one day to visit Valparaíso and Viña del Mar. This will give you enough time to explore both cities and see the main attractions.

- **Take a break.** Valparaíso and Viña del Mar can be a lot to take in, so it's important to take a break every now and then. Find a cafe or restaurant to relax and enjoy the view.

Shopping

Overview of Shopping Options in Santiago

Santiago offers a diverse and exciting array of shopping options that cater to every taste and budget. From bustling markets and modern shopping malls to boutique stores and artisanal shops, Santiago promises a delightful shopping experience for visitors and residents alike. Let's explore the various shopping options that make Santiago a shopper's paradise.

Shopping Malls

Santiago is home to a plethora of modern shopping malls that house both local and international brands. **Parque Arauco, Costanera Center, and Alto Las Condes** are among the largest and most popular malls, boasting an extensive selection of fashion, electronics, home goods, and entertainment options. These malls also feature food courts with a wide variety of cuisines, making them ideal destinations for a full day of shopping and dining.

Boutique Stores in Bellavista

The **bohemian neighborhood of Bellavista** offers an eclectic mix of boutique stores and unique shops. This artistic and cultural hub is a treasure trove of handmade crafts, artistic creations, and one-of-a-kind souvenirs. Visitors can find locally designed clothing, jewelry, and accessories that reflect the vibrant spirit of Santiago's artistic scene.

Mercado Central

For a taste of authentic Chilean culture and culinary delights, **Mercado Central** is a **must-visit** shopping destination. This bustling market, housed in an iconic iron building, is renowned for its fresh seafood and traditional Chilean dishes. Visitors can also find a variety of handicrafts, souvenirs, and local products, making it a perfect place to immerse in the local culture.

Artisan Markets

Santiago boasts several artisan markets, where skilled artisans showcase their craftsmanship and traditional products. The Pueblito Los Dominicos market is a popular spot to find handcrafted pottery, textiles, leather goods, and woodwork, all reflecting Chile's rich cultural heritage. These markets offer a chance to support local artisans and take home unique and meaningful souvenirs.

Luxury Shopping in Vitacura

The upscale neighborhood of Vitacura is renowned for its luxury shopping options, featuring renowned international designer boutiques and high-end brands. El Golf Avenue and Alonso de Córdova Street are the main luxury shopping districts, offering exclusive fashion, jewelry, and accessories for those seeking premium shopping experiences.

Street Markets and Ferias

Throughout Santiago, various street markets and ferias (fairs) offer a lively and vibrant shopping experience. These markets, such as Feria Santa Lucía and Feria Persa Bio-Bio, are known for their diverse offerings, including antiques, vintage clothing, handicrafts, and artisanal food products. Bargaining is a common practice at these markets, adding an element of excitement to the shopping experience.

Mall Vivo Outlet Maipú

For bargain hunters, Mall Vivo Outlet Maipú is a popular destination, offering discounted prices on popular brands. This outlet mall features a wide range of products, including clothing, footwear, and home goods, making it an ideal spot for budget-conscious shoppers looking for quality products at affordable prices.

From upscale luxury boutiques to lively street markets, Santiago's shopping landscape caters to all preferences, providing a diverse and enjoyable shopping experience. Whether you're searching for designer fashion, authentic souvenirs, or unique artisanal creations, the shopping options in Santiago are sure to delight shoppers of all ages and interests.

Popular Shopping Districts and Malls

Here's some information about popular shopping districts and malls in Santiago, Chile:

- **Barrio Lastarria:** This trendy neighborhood is home to a variety of boutiques, art galleries, and cafes. It is located in the heart of Santiago and is a great place to wander around and explore.
- **Bellavista:** This bohemian neighborhood is home to a variety of shops, restaurants, and bars. It is located in the west of Santiago and is a great place to catch live music and people-watch.
- **Barrio Italia:** This Italian-inspired neighborhood is home to a variety of shops, restaurants, and cafes. It is located in the east of Santiago and is a great place to enjoy a leisurely stroll and sample the local cuisine.
- **Parque Arauco:** This is the largest mall in Chile and is located in the Providencia district of Santiago. It has over 400 stores, including international brands such as Zara, H&M, and Nike.
- **Costanera Center:** This is the second-largest mall in Chile and is located in the Vitacura district of Santiago. It has over 300 stores, including international brands such as Louis Vuitton, Gucci, and Prada.
- **Alto Las Condes:** This is a high-end mall located in the Las Condes district of Santiago. It has over 200 stores, including international brands such as Cartier, Rolex, and Hermès.

Here are some tips for shopping in Santiago:

- Bargaining is common in some markets, so don't be afraid to haggle.
- Keep in mind that the prices in Chile are generally higher than in other parts of South America.
- If you're looking for souvenirs, be sure to check out the markets in Barrio Lastarria and Bellavista.
- If you're looking for high-end brands, be sure to visit Parque Arauco or Costanera Center.
- Be sure to bargain if you're buying from street vendors.
- The best time to shop is during the week, when the stores are less crowded.
- If you're planning on doing a lot of shopping, be sure to bring a backpack or large purse to carry your purchases.

Recommendations for Unique Souvenirs and Local Products

Here are some recommendations for unique souvenirs and local products to buy in Santiago, Chile:

- **Copper jewelry:** Copper is a national symbol of Chile, and copper jewelry is a popular souvenir to buy. You can find copper jewelry in a variety of shapes and sizes, from simple earrings and necklaces to elaborate bracelets and rings.

- **Lapis lazuli:** Lapis lazuli is a semi-precious stone that is found in Chile. It is often used in jewelry and other decorative items. You can find lapis lazuli jewelry in a variety of shapes and sizes, from simple pendants to elaborate necklaces and bracelets.

- **Hand-knitted sweaters:** Chile is known for its beautiful hand-knitted sweaters. You can find sweaters in a variety of colors and styles, from simple Aran sweaters to more elaborate Fair Isle sweaters.

- **Pisco:** Pisco is a type of brandy that is made in Chile. It is often enjoyed neat or mixed with other drinks, such as pisco sours. You can buy pisco in most liquor stores in Santiago.

- **Empanadas:** Empanadas are a popular Chilean pastry that is filled with a variety of ingredients, such as meat, cheese, or vegetables. You can find empanadas in most bakeries in Santiago.

- **Chocolate:** Chile is a major producer of chocolate, and you can find a variety of chocolate products in Santiago, from simple bars of chocolate to more elaborate chocolate-covered fruits and nuts.

- **Wine:** Chile is a world-renowned producer of wine, and you can find a variety of wines in Santiago, from inexpensive table wines to expensive fine wines. You can buy wine in most liquor stores in Santiago.

These are just a few ideas for unique souvenirs and local products to buy in Santiago, Chile.

Dining and Nightlife

Local Cuisine and Dining Experiences

Santiago offers a delectable culinary journey that showcases the richness of Chilean cuisine and the fusion of diverse flavors from around the world. From traditional dishes that pay homage to the country's cultural heritage to innovative gastronomic creations, Santiago's dining scene promises a delightful experience for food enthusiasts. Let's explore the local cuisine and dining experiences that make Santiago a true gastronomic delight.

Traditional Chilean Cuisine

Santiago is the perfect place to savor authentic Chilean dishes that reflect the country's culinary traditions. One of the most iconic dishes is the hearty and flavorful Chilean stew known as "Cazuela." This comforting soup is made with meat, potatoes, corn, pumpkin, and other vegetables, simmered to perfection in a savory broth. Another Chilean classic is "Pastel de Choclo," a corn and meat pie that boasts a perfect blend of sweet and savory flavors.

Seafood Delicacies

As a coastal city, Santiago takes pride in its seafood delicacies. "Chupe de Mariscos" is a must-try dish, featuring a delightful combination of seafood, cheese, and corn in a creamy broth. Additionally, "Congrio" (conger eel) is a popular fish found in many Santiago restaurants, often prepared with a flavorful garlic and butter sauce.

Empanadas and Street Food

No culinary journey in Santiago is complete without trying the mouthwatering Chilean empanadas. These savory pastries come in various fillings, such as beef, cheese, chicken, and seafood. Locals and visitors alike enjoy sampling street food in

Santiago, where vendors offer a variety of snacks like "Chorrillana" (a hearty dish of french fries, beef, and onions) and "Completo" (a loaded hot dog topped with avocado, tomato, and mayonnaise).

International Cuisine

Santiago's diverse dining scene also embraces international flavors. Visitors can find restaurants serving a wide range of cuisines, from Italian and Japanese to Mediterranean and Peruvian. This fusion of international influences adds a dynamic and cosmopolitan touch to the city's culinary landscape.

Wine Tasting

Chile is renowned for its exceptional wines, and Santiago provides ample opportunities for wine enthusiasts to indulge in wine tasting experiences. Local wineries offer guided tours and tastings, providing insights into Chile's winemaking traditions and the chance to sample a diverse selection of wines, including the country's famous Carmenere.

Fine Dining and Culinary Excellence

Santiago boasts a thriving fine dining scene, with several restaurants recognized by prestigious international awards. The city's top chefs showcase their culinary prowess by combining local ingredients with innovative techniques to create extraordinary dining experiences.

Cultural Food Markets

Food markets in Santiago, such as Mercado Central and La Vega Central, are vibrant hubs where locals and visitors can savor fresh produce, seafood, and traditional Chilean dishes. These markets offer an authentic glimpse into the city's culinary culture and the opportunity to engage with friendly vendors.

Santiago's culinary landscape is a delightful fusion of traditional flavors, international influences, and innovative creations. Whether you prefer savoring traditional Chilean cuisine, exploring international tastes, or indulging in gourmet experiences, Santiago's dining scene has something to tantalize every palate. The city's passion for food, appreciation for local ingredients, and warm hospitality ensure that dining in Santiago is not just a meal but an unforgettable culinary adventure.

Recommended Restaurants and Cafés

Here are some recommended restaurants and cafes in Santiago, Chile:

Restaurants:

- **La Mar Cebicheria:** This Peruvian ceviche restaurant is a popular spot for locals and tourists alike. The ceviche is fresh and delicious, and the portions are generous.

- **Bistrot 1900:** This French bistro is a great place to enjoy a classic French meal. The food is excellent, and the service is excellent.
- **Happenstance:** This restaurant serves modern Chilean cuisine with a focus on local ingredients. The menu changes seasonally, and the wine list is extensive.
- **Mestizo:** This restaurant serves traditional Chilean dishes with a modern twist. The food is delicious, and the atmosphere is lively.
- **Coya:** This upscale Peruvian restaurant offers a tasting menu of ceviche, tiraditos, and other Peruvian specialties. The food is creative and delicious, and the service is impeccable.

Cafes:

- **La Casona**: This cafe is located in a beautiful old colonial mansion. It serves coffee, tea, pastries, and light meals.
- **La Fuente Alemana:** This cafe is a Santiago institution. It has been serving coffee and pastries since 1875.
- **La Puerta Roja:** This cafe is located in the Bellavista neighborhood. It is a popular spot for people-watching and enjoying a cup of coffee or a glass of wine.
- **Santos Café:** This cafe is located in the Providencia neighborhood. It is a popular spot for working or studying.

- **Creperie La Creperie:** This cafe is located in the Lastarria neighborhood. It serves delicious crepes and waffles.

Nightlife and Entertainment Options

When the sun sets in Santiago, the city comes alive with a vibrant and diverse nightlife that caters to a wide range of tastes and preferences. From lively clubs and bars to cultural performances and entertainment venues, Santiago offers an exciting array of options to keep night owls entertained. Let's explore the nightlife and entertainment scene that makes Santiago an unforgettable destination after dark.

Nightclubs and Bars

Santiago's nightlife is known for its energetic and lively nightclubs and bars, where locals and visitors gather to dance, socialize, and enjoy a memorable night out. The city's nightlife hubs, such as Bellavista and Barrio Brasil, are dotted with trendy bars and clubs that play a mix of music genres, from Latin beats to electronic dance music.

Live Music and Concerts

For music enthusiasts, Santiago offers a diverse range of live music venues that cater to different tastes. From intimate jazz bars to large concert halls, music lovers can indulge in performances that span various genres, including jazz, rock, folk, and Latin rhythms. The city's music scene often hosts both local and international artists, ensuring a dynamic and eclectic experience.

Cultural Performances

Santiago is a city proud of its cultural heritage, and this is evident in the array of cultural performances on offer. Visitors can enjoy traditional dance shows, theater performances, and classical music concerts that celebrate Chile's artistic traditions and creativity.

Rooftop Bars and Terraces

For a more laid-back and sophisticated experience, Santiago boasts a variety of rooftop bars and terraces that provide stunning views of the city's skyline. These elevated venues are the perfect spots to enjoy a cocktail while watching the sunset or reveling in the city's sparkling night lights.

Casinos and Gaming

Santiago's entertainment scene also includes casinos, where visitors can try their luck and enjoy a night of gaming and excitement. The city's casinos offer a mix of slot machines, table games, and live entertainment, creating a thrilling atmosphere for those seeking a bit of nightlife adventure.

Performing Arts and Theaters

The city's theaters and performing arts centers stage a diverse range of productions, from plays and ballet performances to contemporary dance and cultural shows. These venues provide a window into Chile's artistic talent and cultural expression.

Late-Night Dining

After a night of entertainment, Santiago's late-night dining options are sure to satisfy any cravings. From traditional "sanguches" (sandwiches) to international cuisine, the city's eateries and food trucks keep their doors open to cater to hungry night owls.

Whether you're in the mood to dance the night away, enjoy live music, immerse in cultural performances, or simply unwind with a refreshing drink and stunning views, Santiago's nightlife and entertainment options have something for everyone. The city's lively and dynamic nighttime scene ensures that visitors can make the most of their time in Santiago and create lasting memories of the city's vibrant and captivating after-dark atmosphere.

Here's a list of recommended nightlife and entertainment options in Santiago, Chile:

- **Bellavista:** This bohemian neighborhood is home to a variety of bars, restaurants, and clubs. It is located in the west of Santiago and is a great place to catch live music and people-watch.
- **Barrio Italia:** This Italian-inspired neighborhood is home to a variety of bars, restaurants, and cafes. It is located in the east of Santiago and is a great place to enjoy a leisurely stroll and sample the local cuisine.
- **Plaza Baquedano:** This large public square is located in the center of Santiago and is a popular spot for nightlife. There are a number of bars and restaurants located around the square, as well as a number of clubs.
- **Parque Forestal:** This large park is located in the heart of Santiago and is a popular spot for outdoor concerts, theater performances, and other events. There are also a number of bars and restaurants located in the park.
- **Lastarria:** This trendy neighborhood is home to a variety of bars, restaurants, and art galleries. It is located in the heart of Santiago and is a great place to wander around and explore.

Here are some insider tips for enjoying the nightlife in Santiago:

- Bargaining is common in some markets, so don't be afraid to haggle.
- Keep in mind that the prices in Chile are generally higher than in other parts of South America.
- If you're looking for souvenirs, be sure to check out the markets in Barrio Lastarria and Bellavista.
- If you're looking for high-end brands, be sure to visit Parque Arauco or Costanera Center.
- Be sure to bargain if you're buying from street vendors.
- The best time to shop is during the week, when the stores are less crowded.
- If you're planning on doing a lot of shopping, be sure to bring a backpack or large purse to carry your purchases.

Here are some recommended bars and clubs in Santiago:

- **Bar Liguria:** This traditional Chilean bar is located in the Bellavista neighborhood and is a popular spot for locals and tourists alike. The bar serves a variety of Chilean beers and wines, as well as traditional Chilean snacks.
- **Cabildo:** This upscale club is located in the Centro Historico neighborhood and is a popular spot for dancing and live music. The club features a variety of DJs and live bands, and the atmosphere is always lively.
- **La Batuta:** This music venue is located in the Bellavista neighborhood and is a popular spot for concerts and other events. The venue has a capacity of over 2,000

people, and it has hosted a variety of international artists, such as Radiohead, Coldplay, and The Cure.

- **Club Amanda:** This upscale club is located in the Vitacura neighborhood and is a popular spot for dancing and cocktails. The club features a variety of DJs and live bands, and the atmosphere is always sophisticated.

- **Barrio Bar:** This popular bar is located in the Barrio Italia neighborhood and is a great place to enjoy a casual drink and some live music. The bar features a variety of local bands, and the atmosphere is always relaxed and inviting.

Practical
Information

Currency and Money Matters

The official currency of Chile is the **Chilean peso (CLP).** The current exchange rate is approximately 1 USD = 750 CLP.

There are a few different ways to exchange currency in Santiago. You can exchange currency at banks, exchange bureaus, or at the airport. Banks usually offer the best exchange rates, but they may have limited hours of operation. Exchange bureaus are more common and have more flexible hours, but they may not offer the best exchange rates. The airport is a convenient place to exchange currency, but the exchange rates may not be as good as you can find elsewhere.

If you are planning on using a credit or debit card in Santiago, it is important to check with your card issuer to see if there are any foreign transaction fees. Some card issuers charge foreign transaction fees, which can add up quickly.

Here are some tips for saving money on currency exchange in Santiago:

- **Exchange currency at a bank.** Banks usually offer the best exchange rates.
- **Exchange currency at an exchange bureau during off-peak hours.** Exchange bureaus often offer better exchange rates during off-peak hours.
- **Exchange currency at the airport only as a last resort.** The exchange rates at the airport are usually not as good as you can find elsewhere.
- **Use a credit card that does not charge foreign transaction fees.** This can save you a lot of money in the long run.

Here are some important things to keep in mind about currency and money matters in Santiago:

- The Chilean peso is a relatively weak currency. This means that your money will go further in Chile than it would in other countries.
- It is not necessary to exchange all of your currency into Chilean pesos. You can use credit and debit cards in most places in Santiago.
- It is a good idea to have some Chilean pesos on hand for small purchases and tipping.
- You can exchange currency at most banks and exchange bureaus in Santiago.
- Some banks and exchange bureaus charge foreign transaction fees.
- It is a good idea to check with your credit or debit card issuer to see if they charge foreign transaction fees.

Safety Tips and Emergency Contacts

Safety Tips

- **Be aware of your surroundings.** Do not walk alone at night, and be sure to keep your belongings close to you.
- **Don't flash your valuables.** This could attract thieves.
- **Be careful when using ATMs.** Make sure to use ATMs that are located in well-lit areas.

- If you are lost, ask a police officer or a local for directions.
- Keep your passport and other important documents in a safe place.
- Be aware of the local laws and customs.

Emergency Contacts

- **Police:** 133
- **Ambulance:** 131
- **Fire Department:** 132

Here are some additional tips for staying safe in Santiago:

- If you are a woman traveling alone, be sure to let someone know where you are going and when you expect to be back.
- If you are planning on going hiking or camping, be sure to let someone know where you are going and when you expect to be back.
- If you are driving, be sure to be aware of the local traffic laws.
- Be sure to drink plenty of water, especially if you are hiking or camping.
- Be sure to pack sunscreen, a hat, and sunglasses.
- If you are feeling sick, be sure to seek medical attention immediately.

Language and Communication

Language and communication are fundamental aspects of human interaction and play a crucial role in shaping societies and cultures. In Santiago, as in the rest of Chile, language is an integral part of daily life, and understanding the nuances of communication can enhance one's experience in the city. Let's explore the language and communication in Santiago and the cultural significance it holds.

Official Language

The official language of Chile is Spanish, and Santiago is no exception. Spanish is the primary language used in all aspects of life, including business, education, government, and social interactions. While many locals may understand and speak English to some extent, especially in tourist areas, having a basic knowledge of Spanish can greatly enrich the communication experience in Santiago.

Chilean Spanish

Chilean Spanish has its unique characteristics and colloquial expressions that set it apart from standard Spanish spoken in other Spanish-speaking countries. Visitors may encounter Chilean slang, known as "Chilenismos," which includes different words and phrases used in everyday conversations. Embracing and understanding these local nuances can foster better communication and cultural integration.

Friendliness and Warmth

Chileans are generally known for their friendliness and warm hospitality. Locals appreciate visitors who attempt to communicate in Spanish, even if it's just a few basic phrases. A friendly attitude and a willingness to engage with the local language can lead to meaningful interactions and connections with the people of Santiago.

Non-Verbal Communication

Non-verbal communication also plays a significant role in Santiago's culture. Chileans often use hand gestures, facial expressions, and body language to convey emotions and intentions. While some gestures may be universally understood, others may have specific meanings in the local context. Observing and adopting these non-verbal cues can aid in effective communication and cultural understanding.

Respect for Formality

Chilean culture places value on formality and respect in communication, especially when addressing elders or authority figures. Using formal pronouns and polite expressions demonstrates courtesy and is appreciated in social and professional settings. However, as interactions become more familiar and casual, locals may transition to informal language.

Language Exchange

Language exchange opportunities abound in Santiago, where locals and international visitors gather to practice different languages. Joining language exchange events or conversation groups can provide a supportive environment for improving language skills and forging connections with people from diverse backgrounds.

Embracing Multilingualism

Santiago's cultural diversity is reflected in the presence of various languages spoken by the city's diverse population. Besides Spanish, you may encounter speakers of indigenous languages like Mapudungun and Aymara, as well as people from different countries conversing in their native tongues. Embracing this multilingualism fosters cultural appreciation and respect for linguistic diversity.

Language and communication are bridges that connect individuals and communities, and in Santiago, they play an integral role in building relationships and understanding the local culture. Embracing the Spanish language, appreciating Chilean expressions, and engaging in meaningful communication can enrich one's experience in Santiago, fostering lasting connections and a deeper appreciation for the city's unique cultural tapestry.

Local Customs and Etiquette

Understanding and respecting local customs and etiquette is essential when visiting Santiago. As a city deeply rooted in cultural traditions, Santiago's customs and manners play a significant role in daily life and interactions. Embracing these practices not only enhances your travel experience but also fosters meaningful connections with the local community. **Here are some key customs and etiquette to keep in mind while in Santiago:**

Greetings and Personal Space: Chileans are warm and welcoming, often greeting with a handshake or a kiss on the cheek for close acquaintances. When meeting someone for the first time, a firm handshake is the appropriate greeting. Remember that Chileans value personal space, so maintaining an appropriate distance during conversations is appreciated.

Use of Formal Language: Santiago adheres to a sense of formality in communication. Using titles and last names when addressing strangers or elders is customary and considered a sign of respect. As you become more acquainted with locals, you may transition to using first names in casual settings.

Punctuality and Flexibility: Chileans generally appreciate punctuality for formal events and business meetings. However, in social settings, such as gatherings with friends or family, it's common for events to start a bit later than the scheduled time. Being flexible and understanding about timing in social situations is considered polite.

Dining Etiquette: Chileans have a strong culture of sharing meals, and dining etiquette is an important aspect of their customs. When invited to someone's home for a meal, it's customary to bring a small gift, such as a bottle of wine or dessert. During the meal, wait until the host begins eating before you start, and try a bit of everything served as a sign of appreciation for the culinary experience.

Respect for Elders: Chileans hold great respect for their elders, and it's essential to show consideration and deference to older individuals. Offering your seat on public transport to elderly people is a kind gesture that is greatly appreciated.

Dress Code: Santiago is a city where appearances matter, so dressing neatly and conservatively in public places, especially in religious sites, is recommended. Beachwear is appropriate only at the beach or poolside, not in city streets or restaurants.

Tipping and Gratuities: Tipping is not mandatory in Chile, but leaving a gratuity for good service is a common practice. A 10% tip at restaurants is generally appreciated, and it's customary to round up the fare when using taxis.

Photography Etiquette: Before taking photographs of people, especially strangers, it's polite to ask for permission first. Respecting individuals' privacy and cultural beliefs is paramount when capturing moments in public spaces.

Transportation Options for Day Trips and Excursions

When exploring Santiago and its surrounding areas, various transportation options are available for day trips and excursions, each offering unique advantages to suit different preferences and destinations. From convenience and comfort to cost-effectiveness and flexibility, these transportation choices make it easy for travelers to embark on memorable adventures. Let's explore the transportation options for day trips and excursions from Santiago.

Private Tours and Transfers

For a hassle-free and personalized experience, private tours and transfers are an excellent option. Many tour operators offer tailored excursions to popular destinations like the Maipo Valley, Valparaíso, and Viña del Mar. With a private tour, you can customize your itinerary, travel at your own pace, and have the undivided attention of a knowledgeable guide.

Rental Cars

For travelers seeking independence and flexibility, renting a car allows you to explore Santiago's surrounding areas at your own convenience. Rental car agencies are readily available in the city, offering a range of vehicle options to accommodate different group sizes and budgets. However, it's essential to consider

Santiago's traffic conditions and parking availability when opting for this choice.

Metro and Buses

Santiago's efficient public transportation system, including the metro and buses, provides an economical way to reach nearby destinations for day trips. For instance, you can take the metro to Viña del Mar or Valparaíso, both approximately two hours away from Santiago. Buses are another reliable and cost-effective option for excursions to destinations with less direct metro access.

Regional Trains

The regional train network connects Santiago with nearby towns, making it a convenient option for exploring the countryside. For instance, you can take a train to San Antonio or Rancagua for a day trip to experience Chile's rural charm and local culture.

Tour Buses

Tour buses and organized day tours are popular choices for travelers who prefer a guided experience with like-minded companions. These tours offer a structured itinerary and the expertise of knowledgeable guides, taking you to popular attractions and providing valuable insights along the way.

Bicycle Tours

For the adventurous and eco-conscious travelers, bicycle tours are an excellent way to explore Santiago's outskirts and nearby regions. Several tour operators offer cycling excursions, providing an active and immersive experience while appreciating the scenic landscapes and local charm.

Shared Transfers

Shared transfers are a budget-friendly option for day trips and excursions. Many tour operators offer shared shuttle services to popular destinations, allowing you to split the cost with other travelers while still enjoying a comfortable ride.

Each transportation option has its unique appeal, allowing you to tailor your day trips and excursions to match your preferences and interests. Whether you prefer the convenience of private tours, the flexibility of rental cars, or the camaraderie of group tours, Santiago's array of transportation choices ensures that you can embark on unforgettable journeys and create cherished memories during your time in Chile.

Additional Tips & Recommendations

Packing Essentials

Here is a list of packing essentials for a trip to Santiago, Chile:

- **Comfortable shoes:** You will be doing a lot of walking in Santiago, so it is important to pack comfortable shoes.
- **Lightweight clothing:** The weather in Santiago is mild year-round, so you will mostly need to pack lightweight clothing.
- **A raincoat:** It can rain in Santiago at any time of year, so it is a good idea to pack a raincoat.
- **Sunscreen:** The sun in Santiago can be strong, so it is important to pack sunscreen.
- **Hat and sunglasses:** A hat and sunglasses will help you protect yourself from the sun.
- **A backpack:** A backpack is a good way to carry your belongings while you are exploring Santiago.

- **A water bottle:** It is important to stay hydrated, so be sure to pack a water bottle.
- **A camera:** Santiago is a beautiful city, and you will want to capture your memories with a camera.
- **Travel insurance:** Travel insurance can help you protect yourself in case of an emergency.

Here are some additional tips for packing for a trip to Santiago:

- Pack layers: The weather in Santiago can change quickly, so it is a good idea to pack layers that you can add or remove as needed.
- Pack clothes that are appropriate for the activities you plan on doing. If you are planning on doing a lot of hiking, for example, you will need to pack different clothes than if you are planning on spending most of your time in the city.
- Don't forget to pack any medications you take regularly.
- If you are traveling from a country with a different electrical outlet, be sure to pack an adapter.
- If you are traveling with a laptop or other electronic devices, be sure to pack the necessary chargers.
- If you are traveling with valuables, be sure to pack them in your carry-on luggage.

Useful Phrases in Spanish

Learning a few useful phrases in Spanish can greatly enhance your travel experience in Santiago and throughout Chile. While many locals in Santiago speak some English, making an effort to communicate in Spanish will be appreciated and can lead to more meaningful interactions. Here are some essential phrases to help you get started:

Greetings

- Hello / Hi - Hola
- Good morning - Buenos días
- Good afternoon / Good evening - Buenas tardes
- Good night - Buenas noches
- How are you? - ¿Cómo estás? (informal) / ¿Cómo está usted? (formal)

Basic Expressions

- Yes - Sí
- No - No
- Please - Por favor
- Thank you - Gracias
- You're welcome - De nada
- Excuse me / I'm sorry - Perdón / Disculpe

Introductions

- My name is [Name] - Mi nombre es [Nombre]
- What's your name? - ¿Cómo te llamas? (informal) / ¿Cómo se llama usted? (formal)
- Nice to meet you - Mucho gusto

Asking for Help

- Can you help me? - ¿Me puedes ayudar? (informal) / ¿Me puede ayudar? (formal)
- Where is [place]? - ¿Dónde está [lugar]?
- I don't understand - No entiendo
- Could you speak more slowly, please? - ¿Puedes hablar más despacio, por favor?

Ordering Food and Drinks

- I would like... - Me gustaría...
- What do you recommend? - ¿Qué recomiendas?
- The bill, please - La cuenta, por favor
- Cheers! - ¡Salud!

Shopping

- How much is this? - ¿Cuánto cuesta esto?
- I'm just looking - Solo estoy mirando
- Can I pay with a credit card? - ¿Puedo pagar con tarjeta de crédito?

Directions

- Where is the [place]? - ¿Dónde está [lugar]?
- Go straight - Ve derecho
- Turn left / right - Gira a la izquierda / derecha
- It's on the left / right - Está a la izquierda / derecha
- Is it far from here? - ¿Está lejos de aquí?

Emergencies

- Help! - ¡Ayuda!
- I need a doctor - Necesito un médico
- Call the police - Llama a la policía

Remember, don't be afraid to use these phrases even if your Spanish is not perfect. Locals in Santiago will appreciate your effort and be more than willing to help you along the way. Being polite and respectful while using these phrases will go a long way in making your experience in Santiago enjoyable and rewarding. *¡Buena suerte! (Good luck!)*

Recommended Books, Movies, and Music

Recommended Books

1. *The House of the Spirits* by Isabel Allende - A captivating family saga set in Chile, weaving magical realism with

historical events, offering a unique insight into the country's turbulent past.

2. *My Invented Country* by Isabel Allende - A memoir by the renowned Chilean author, reflecting on her life, family, and the essence of Chilean culture and identity.

3. *2666* by Roberto Bolaño - Though set mainly in Mexico, this epic novel by the Chilean author explores the dark underbelly of society and the human condition, making it a compelling read for literature enthusiasts.

4. *The Posthumous Memoirs of Bras Cubas* by Machado de Assis - A classic novel from Brazilian literature, written by one of Latin America's most celebrated authors, offering a witty and satirical exploration of life and society.

5. *The Motorcycle Diaries* by Ernesto "Che" Guevara - This travelogue details the transformative journey of the young Che Guevara through South America, including his experiences in Chile.

Recommended Movies

1. *No* (2012) - A powerful political drama based on the true story of the 1988 Chilean referendum to determine whether Pinochet's rule should continue or not, showcasing the impact of advertising and democracy.

2. *Gloria* (2013) - A heartfelt Chilean film portraying the life of a free-spirited woman in her 50s, exploring themes of independence and self-discovery.

3. *City of God* (2002) - A Brazilian crime drama that follows the lives of two young boys growing up in a violent favela in Rio de Janeiro, offering a raw and compelling look into Brazilian society.

4. *Central Station* (1998) - A Brazilian drama about the unlikely friendship between an elderly woman and a young boy, exploring themes of redemption and human connection.

5. *Wild Tales* (2014) - An Argentine-Spanish anthology film comprising six darkly comedic stories that examine the human condition and societal frustrations.

Recommended Music

1. ***Violeta Parra*** - An iconic Chilean folk singer-songwriter and artist, known for her poetic lyrics and contributions to the Nueva Canción Chilena movement.

2. ***Café Tacvba*** - A Mexican rock band renowned for their innovative sound, blending rock, alternative, and traditional Mexican influences.

3. ***Jorge Drexler*** - A Uruguayan singer-songwriter and musician whose music often combines folk, rock, and electronic elements, earning him international acclaim.

4. ***Caetano Veloso*** - A Brazilian musician and songwriter, considered one of the pioneers of Tropicalismo, a musical movement that merged traditional Brazilian music with rock and pop.

5. ***Ana Tijoux*** - A Chilean-French musician known for her thought-provoking rap lyrics and socially conscious themes.

These books, movies, and music selections offer a glimpse into the rich cultural heritage and diverse artistic expressions of Latin America. Whether you're looking to immerse yourself in literature, explore cinematic narratives, or discover the rhythmic melodies of the region, these recommendations will undoubtedly provide a captivating and enriching experience.

Sustainable and Responsible Travel Practices

Sustainable and responsible travel practices are becoming increasingly important in today's world, as travelers seek to minimize their impact on the environment, respect local cultures, and support the well-being of local communities. By adopting these practices, travelers can make a positive difference and contribute to the preservation of natural and cultural treasures for future generations. Here are some key sustainable and responsible travel practices to consider:

Choose Eco-Friendly Accommodations: Opt for accommodations that prioritize sustainability, such as eco-lodges, green hotels, or properties with certifications like LEED (Leadership in Energy and Environmental Design). These establishments often implement energy-efficient practices, waste reduction measures, and support local conservation initiatives.

Reduce Plastic Waste: Bring a reusable water bottle and refill it from safe water sources to reduce single-use plastic waste. Avoid accepting plastic straws and utensils when dining out and dispose of waste properly, recycling whenever possible.

Support Local Communities: Engage with local businesses, artisans, and restaurants, and support their products and services. This helps create a positive economic impact, empowering local communities and preserving traditional practices.

Respect Local Cultures and Customs: Take the time to learn about the local culture, traditions, and customs before your visit. Show respect by dressing modestly where appropriate and being mindful of cultural norms, especially when visiting religious sites.

Conserve Water and Energy: Practice water and energy conservation during your travels. Turn off lights and air conditioning when leaving your room, reuse towels and linens, and take shorter showers to minimize water consumption.

Choose Sustainable Tour Operators: Select tour operators and guides that prioritize responsible and sustainable tourism practices. Look for operators who contribute to environmental conservation, respect wildlife, and support local communities.

Opt for Public Transportation and Walking: Use public transportation, such as buses or trains, whenever possible, to reduce carbon emissions from private vehicles. Explore cities on foot or by bike to experience the local atmosphere and reduce your environmental footprint.

Engage in Responsible Wildlife Tourism: Avoid engaging in activities that harm or exploit wildlife. Refrain from supporting attractions that involve animal performances or allow close interactions with wild animals. Instead, choose responsible wildlife encounters that prioritize the well-being of animals in their natural habitats.

Dispose of Waste Responsibly: Avoid leaving behind litter or waste while exploring natural areas. Use designated trash bins and recycling facilities, and if necessary, carry a small bag to collect and dispose of waste responsibly.

Offset Your Carbon Footprint: Consider offsetting the carbon emissions from your travels by supporting carbon offset projects that help reduce greenhouse gas emissions and promote sustainable practices.

Conclusion

Rediscover Santiago, Chile

As we come to the end of this captivating journey through the pages of "Loquetrip's Santiago, Chile Travel Guide 2024," we invite you to peel back the layers of this dynamic metropolis and immerse yourself in its rich history, vibrant culture, and breathtaking landscapes.

Santiago's heritage, interwoven with stories of conquest, resilience, and rebirth, reveals itself in splendid architecture and charming cafes in Barrio Lastarria and the artistic expressions of Bellavista. The city's culinary odyssey tantalizes taste buds with delectable seafood at Mercado Central and mouthwatering empanadas from local vendors, all accompanied by world-class Chilean wines.

Nestled amidst the Andes mountains, Santiago's natural splendors captivate with stunning views from Santa Lucía Hill and the lush greenery of Santiago Metropolitan Park. As you embrace local traditions during vibrant festivals like Fiestas

Patrias and Semana Santa, you'll feel the pulse of Santiago's beating heart.

Throughout this journey, we encourage you to be mindful of the impact you leave behind. Embrace sustainable and responsible travel practices, support local artisans and businesses, and cherish the beauty of Santiago with a heart of stewardship for the environment and communities you encounter.

This book is an invitation to forge new memories, to fall in love with its authenticity, and to leave a part of your soul in this captivating city. Whether sipping a café con piernas, exploring world-class museums, or strolling through picturesque plazas, Santiago's heart will forever resonate within you.

As you set out to rediscover Santiago, may you find inspiration in the moments of awe, shared laughter, and the warmth of its people. The spirit of Santiago has an uncanny ability to ignite the passion of the traveler's soul and awaken the sense of wonder that resides in us all.

Prepare to embark on this extraordinary adventure of rediscovery. Santiago awaits with open arms, ready to reveal its hidden treasures and unlock the magic that lies within. Rediscover Santiago, and in the process, rediscover a part of yourselves that you never knew existed.

Embrace the Culture and History of the City

Santiago is not merely a place; it is a living, breathing tapestry of stories, traditions, and the remarkable resilience of its people.

A Journey through Time

The streets of Santiago bear witness to the passage of time, with each corner telling a tale of its own. Explore the heart of the city at Plaza de Armas, where the pulse of Santiago can be felt in the bustling atmosphere, and the magnificent Metropolitan Cathedral stands tall as a testament to the city's spiritual heritage. As you stroll through the historic neighborhoods, the echoes of the past intertwine with the vibrant present, creating a mesmerizing harmony.

The Spirit of Art and Expression

In Santiago, art transcends beyond the confines of galleries, infusing itself into every aspect of daily life. Uncover the enchanting street art that adorns the city's walls, where graffiti artists transform urban spaces into captivating canvases of self-expression. Immerse yourself in the world of literature, as Santiago has been a muse to renowned writers like Pablo Neruda and Isabel Allende, leaving an indelible mark on the literary landscape.

Music, Dance, and Festivals

Santiago's beating heart is infused with the rhythm of music and dance. From the spirited steps of the cueca during Fiestas Patrias to the captivating performances of traditional folklore, the city's festivals celebrate the soul of Chilean culture. Join in the merriment, let the music move your feet, and experience the exhilaration of being part of something greater than yourself.

Preserving Traditions and Heritage

As you delve deeper into Santiago's culture, you'll discover a profound respect for traditions and an unwavering commitment to preserving the city's heritage. Step into the beautiful courtyards of Bellavista and the historic homes-turned-museums, and you'll find that every brick and beam carries the weight of the past, holding within it stories that connect generations.

A City of Warmth and Connection

Beyond its stunning architecture and natural wonders, Santiago's true allure lies in the warmth of its people. The locals, known for their genuine hospitality, will welcome you with open arms, eager to share their customs, stories, and laughter. Engage with them, learn from their wisdom, and be part of their embrace that makes you feel at home, even in a foreign land.

A Timeless Love Affair

As you conclude this enchanting journey through Santiago, you'll come to realize that the bond you've forged with the city goes beyond a fleeting visit. Santiago becomes a part of you, a timeless love affair that lives on in the memories you've made and the experiences you've cherished.

So, dear explorers, as you embrace the culture and history of Santiago, let the city leave an indelible mark on your heart. *Let its stories become your stories, its rhythms become your rhythms, and its soul become an inseparable part of yours.* As you bid farewell to Santiago, know that it will forever welcome you back, ready to unfold new chapters of discovery whenever you choose to return.

Thank you for allowing us to be your guides on this unforgettable journey through the culture and history of Santiago, Chile. May the spirit of this vibrant city continue to inspire you as you continue your adventures across the globe. Until we meet again, Santiago's heart beats within you, an enduring reminder of the magic you have encountered in this remarkable place. Safe travels, and may the love for travel and exploration guide you always.

fond adieu

Thanks for reading! Please add a short review on Amazon and let us know your thought!

We hope you enjoyed our guide! If you did, we would appreciate it if you would leave a review on Amazon. You can also follow us on social media – X and Instagram (@LoquetripGuide) and tag us in your photos from your trip. We love seeing our guides in action!

Made in United States
Troutdale, OR
02/20/2024